Pat Mora

WHO WROTE THAT?

LOUISA MAY ALCOTT
JANE AUSTEN
AVI
JUDY BLUME
BETSY BYARS
BEVERLY CLEARY
ROBERT CORMIER
BRUCE COVILLE
ROALD DAHL
CHARLES DICKENS
THEODOR GEISEL
WILL HOBBS
ANTHONY HOROWITZ
GAIL CARSON LEVINE
C.S. LEWIS
ANN M. MARTIN
L.M. MONTGOMERY
PAT MORA
SCOTT O'DELL
BARBARA PARK
GARY PAULSEN
TAMORA PIERCE
EDGAR ALLAN POE
BEATRIX POTTER
PHILIP PULLMAN
MYTHMAKER: THE STORY OF J.K. ROWLING
MAURICE SENDAK
R.L. STINE
EDWARD L. STRATEMEYER
E.B. WHITE
LAURA INGALLS WILDER
JANE YOLEN

Pat Mora

Hal Marcovitz

**Foreword by
Kyle Zimmer**

South Huntington Pub. Lib.
145 Pidgeon Hill Rd.
Huntington Sta., N.Y. 11746

Pat Mora

Copyright © 2008 by Infobase Publishing

All rights reserved. No part of this book may be reproduced or utilized in any form or by any means, electronic or mechanical, including photocopying, recording, or by any information storage or retrieval systems, without permission in writing from the publisher. For information contact:

Chelsea House
An imprint of Infobase Publishing
132 West 31st Street
New York NY 10001

Library of Congress Cataloging-in-Publication Data
Marcovitz, Hal.
 Pat Mora / Hal Marcovitz.
  p. cm. — (Who wrote that?)
 Includes bibliographical references and index.
 ISBN-13: 978-0-7910-9528-7 (acid-free paper)
 ISBN-10: 0-7910-9528-2 (acid-free paper) 1. Mora, Pat—Juvenile literature. 2. Poets, American—20th century—Biography—Juvenile literature. 3. Mexican American authors—Biography—Juvenile literature. 4. Mexican American women—Biography—Juvenile literature. 5. Children's literature—Authorship—Juvenile literature. I. Title.
 PS3563.O73Z77 2007
 811'.54—dc22
 [B]   2007019452

Chelsea House books are available at special discounts when purchased in bulk quantities for business, associations, institutions, or sales promotions. Please call our Special Sales Department in New York at (212) 967-8800 or (800) 322-8755.

You can find Chelsea House on the World Wide Web at http://www.chelseahouse.com

Text design by Keith Trego and Erika Arroyo
Cover design by Keith Trego and Jooyoung An

Printed in the United States of America

Bang EJB 10 9 8 7 6 5 4 3 2 1

This book is printed on acid-free paper.

All links and Web addresses were checked and verified to be correct at the time of publication. Because of the dynamic nature of the Web, some addresses and links may have changed since publication and may no longer be valid.

Table of Contents

FOREWORD BY
KYLE ZIMMER
PRESIDENT, FIRST BOOK — 6

1 AUNT LOBO — 11

2 A WRITER EMERGES — 21

3 LIVING ON THE BORDER — 39

4 THE WRITER IS A GARDENER — 51

5 THE MAKING OF A POET — 63

6 STORIES ABOUT WOMEN — 75

7 STORIES ABOUT FAMILIES — 87

8 PROMOTING LITERACY IN AMERICA — 99

CHRONOLOGY — 112
NOTES — 114
WORKS BY PAT MORA — 117
POPULAR BOOKS — 119
POPULAR CHARACTERS — 121
MAJOR AWARDS — 122
BIBLIOGRAPHY — 125
FURTHER READING — 128
INDEX — 130

WHO WROTE THAT?

FOREWORD BY
KYLE ZIMMER
PRESIDENT, FIRST BOOK

HUMANITY IS POWERED by stories. From our earliest days as thinking beings, we employed every available tool to tell each other stories. We danced, drew pictures on the walls of our caves, spoke, and sang. All of this extraordinary effort was designed to entertain, recount the news of the day, explain natural occurrences—and then gradually to build religious and cultural traditions and establish the common bonds and continuity that eventually formed civilizations. Stories are the most powerful force in the universe; they are the primary element that has distinguished our evolutionary path.

Our love of the story has not diminished with time. Enormous segments of societies are devoted to the art of storytelling. Book sales in the United States alone topped $26 billion last year; movie studios spend fortunes to create and promote stories; and the news industry is more pervasive in its presence than ever before.

There is no mystery to our fascination. Great stories are magic. They can introduce us to new cultures or remind us of the nobility and failures of our own; inspire us to greatness or scare us to death; but above all, stories provide human insight on a level that is unavailable through any other source. In fact, stories connect each of us to the rest of humanity not just in our own time, but also throughout history.

FOREWORD

This special magic of books is the greatest treasure that we can hand down from generation to generation. In fact, that spark in a child that comes from books became the motivation for the creation of my organization, First Book, a national literacy program with a simple mission: to provide new books to the most disadvantaged children. First Book has been at work in hundreds of communities for over a decade. Every year, children in need receive millions of books through our organization, and millions more are provided through dedicated literacy institutions across the United States and around the world. In addition, groups of people dedicate themselves tirelessly to working with children to share reading and stories in every imaginable setting from schools to the streets. Of course, this Herculean effort serves many important goals. Literacy translates to productivity and employability in life and many other valid and even essential elements. But at the heart of this movement are people who love stories, love to read, and want desperately to ensure that no one misses the wonderful possibilities that reading provides.

When thinking about the importance of books, there is an overwhelming urge to cite the literary devotion of great minds. Some have written of the magnitude of the importance of literature. Amy Lowell, an American poet, captured the concept when she said, "Books are more than books. They are the life, the very heart and core of ages past, the reason why men lived and worked and died, the essence and quintessence of their lives." Others have spoken of their personal obsession with books, as in Thomas Jefferson's simple statement: "I live for books." But more compelling, perhaps, is the almost instinctive excitement in children for books and stories.

Throughout my years at First Book, I have heard truly extraordinary stories about the power of books in the lives of children. In one case, a homeless child, who had been bounced from one location to another, later resurfaced—and the only possession that he had fought to keep was the book he was given as part of a First Book distribution months earlier. More recently, I met a child who, upon receiving the book he wanted, flashed a big smile and said, "This is my big chance!" These snapshots reveal the true power of books and stories to give hope and change lives.

As these children grow up and continue to develop their love of reading, they will owe a profound debt to those volunteers who reached out to them—a debt that they may repay by reaching out to spark the next generation of readers. But there is a greater debt owed by all of us—a debt to the storytellers, the authors, who have bound us together, inspired our leaders, fueled our civilizations, and helped us put our children to sleep with their heads full of images and ideas.

WHO WROTE THAT? is a series of books dedicated to introducing us to a few of these incredible individuals. While we have almost always honored stories, we have not uniformly honored storytellers. In fact, some of the most important authors have toiled in complete obscurity throughout their lives or have been openly persecuted for the uncomfortable truths that they have laid before us. When confronted with the magnitude of their written work, we can forget that writers are people. They struggle through the same daily indignities and dental appointments, and they experience the intense joy and bottomless despair that many of us do. Yet, somehow they rise above it all to weave a powerful thread that connects us all. It is a rare honor to have the opportunity that these books provide to share the lives of these extraordinary people. Enjoy.

Young Pat Mora poses with her father, Raúl Antonio Mora, and the family dog, Cadet, in front of their stone house at 704 Mesita Street in El Paso, Texas.

1

Aunt Lobo

WHEN CHILDREN'S BOOK author and poet Pat Mora was a young girl growing up in El Paso, Texas, her family shared their home with an aunt, Ignacia Delgado Manquera, whom all the children in the family called "Lobo." Mora later explained that in Spanish, *lobo* means "wolf," which was "an odd name for a generous and loving aunt. Like all names, it became synonymous with her, and to this day returns me to my childself. Although the name seemed perfectly natural to us and to our friends, it did cause frowns from strangers throughout the years." (*Authors in Depth*, p. 31)

According to Mora, her aunt Lobo actually earned her nickname. Each night, when she arrived home from work, Lobo would summon the children in the Mora home by calling out, *"¿Dónde están mis lobitos?"* which means, "Where are my little wolves?" (*Authors in Depth*, p. 31) The children, in turn, started to call their *tía* (aunt) Lobo.

Years later, as Mora became one of the country's leading Latino voices in poetry and children's literature, she would often draw on the personal experiences from her childhood in El Paso as inspiration. In 1992, Mora published her first children's book, *A Birthday Basket for Tía*. The story tells how a young girl named Cecilia searches for a ninetieth birthday present for her great-aunt. With the help of her cat Chica, Cecilia fills a basket with reminders of the good times she has shared with Tía: a mixing bowl they use to make cookies; a red ball they use to play catch; a flowerpot for the flowers they grow together; a cup for the mint tea that Tía makes for Cecilia when she is ill; and a book that Tía reads to Cecilia. In the story, Cecilia says,

> Mamá is cooking for the surprise party. I smell beans bubbling on the stove. Mamá is cutting fruit—pineapple, watermelon, mangoes. I sit in the backyard and watch Chica chase butterflies. I hear bees bzzzzz.
>
> I draw pictures in the sand with a stick. I draw a picture of my aunt, my *Tía*. I say, "Chica, what will we give Tía?" (*A Birthday Basket for Tía*)

At the end of the story, when Cecilia gives the basket to Tía, the older woman is overjoyed. She tosses aside her cane so she can dance with Cecilia. "Everyone laughs,"

Cecilia says. "Then the music starts and my aunt surprises me. She takes my hand in hers. Without her cane, she starts to dance with me." (*A Birthday Basket for Tía*)

Book critics praised *A Birthday Basket for Tía*. The national trade magazine of the book publishing industry, *Publishers Weekly*, called it a "poignant picture book" and said "Mora's text flows smoothly from one event to the next, and clearly presents the careful planning behind Cecilia's gift-gathering mission. Repetition of the items inside the basket and the occasional use of Spanish words are helpful reinforcements for young readers."[1] Meanwhile, a reviewer for *Horn Book*, a magazine that covers the children's book publishing industry, said Mora's book was an "honest, child-centered story . . . [that] exemplifies the best of recent multicultural publishing."[2]

SPARK OF THE STORYTELLER

According to Mora, she owes a very large debt to her aunt Lobo, who passed on the spark of the storyteller. Each evening, Lobo would gather the four Mora children around her and tell them stories, both in Spanish and in English, about life in old Mexico, which Lobo and her family left in 1915. Mora described her aunt:

> This aunt, Ignacia Delgado, the star of my first children's book, *A Birthday Basket for Tía,* was a wonderful storyteller. She'd sit on the edge of our beds and in Spanish tell us about when she was a little girl in Mexico, about the time she was punished and ate all the candy that was cooling in the room next to the classroom. Her voice, like a magic Spanish carpet, carried me back with her."[3]

Lobo was the oldest half-sister of Mora's mother, Estela. They were daughters of a judge who fled Mexico to escape the violence of the Mexican Revolution. When her family made the decision to flee, Lobo was a young woman, and Estela was not yet born. The Delgado family had to leave most of their possessions behind, so when Lobo arrived in the United States, she had to learn English and seek a job.

Soon, Lobo found employment in an El Paso department store selling sheets, pillowcases, and tablecloths. She never married, and as Lobo grew older, she moved in with Estela's young family to help her half-sister raise her four children: Pat Mora, her two sisters, and a brother. Mora recalled,

> Lobo saved her money to take us out to dinner and a movie, to take us to Los Angeles in the summer, to buy us shiny black shoes for Christmas. Though she never married and never bore children, Lobo taught me much about one of our greatest challenges as human beings: loving well. I don't think she ever discussed the subject with me, but through the years she lived her love, and I was privileged to watch. (*Authors in Depth*, p. 33)

One story that Mora learned from Lobo was how she celebrated *El Día de los Muertos,* or All Souls' Day, which is observed in Mexico on November 2. To commemorate the holiday, Mexicans visit the cemeteries where their dead relatives are buried, and they care for their gravesites: They clean the tombstones, pull weeds from the gravesites, and plant fresh flowers. According to Lobo, she would rise before dawn on All Souls' Day,

AUNT LOBO

When Pat was growing up, her aunt, Ignacia Delgado Manquera (above), lived with the Mora family. The children called their aunt Lobo and were exceptionally fond of her. In Mora's first book for children, A Birthday Basket for Tía, *the titular aunt is based on Aunt Lobo.*

Did you know...

Did you know that *A Birthday Basket for Tía* is more than just the story of Pat Mora's aunt Lobo? In the book, Mora based the character of Cecilia on her own daughter, Cecilia, who is also known as Cissy. At the time the book was written, Cecilia was a little girl who loved cats, which is why Mora included the mischievous cat, Chica, in the story. Today, Cecilia Burnside is a veterinarian in Austin, Texas, who specializes in the treatment of cats. Mora also has two other children, Bill Burnside and Libby Martinez.

Mora's children and other members of her family have served as characters in some of her storybooks or have been the subjects of her poetry. For example, in the poem "To My Son," Mora wrote about the pain of watching Bill grow up.

According to Mora, her children may have experienced some uncomfortable moments when her poetry has revealed her feelings about them. She explained,

> I think that since one of the things that poetry does is reveal a lot, children have very mixed feelings about their parents' revealing that much; so I think most of their lives they will view my writing out of the corner of their eyes, because they won't want to know too much about that more personal side of me.*

* Quoted in William Balassi, John F. Crawford, and Annie O. Eysturoy, eds. *This Is About Vision: Interviews With Southwestern Writers.* Albuquerque: University of New Mexico Press, 1990, p. 135.

"dressing carefully in black, wanting *mis muerotos* (my dead ones) to be proud of me, proud to have me looking respectable and proud to have their graves taken care of." (*Authors in Depth*, p. 33)

Lobo's stories contained many details. For the story about All Souls' Day, Lobo recalled the aroma of her perfume, the scent of the chrysanthemums she carried to the gravesites, and even the breakfast she ate before she made the trip across town to the cemetery. Even though Lobo was more than 90 years old, her mind remained sharp, and she had little trouble recalling those details for Mora. Later, when Mora became a storyteller, she included similar details about the lives of her characters in her books and poems.

Lobo truly did dance on her ninetieth birthday. In her poem "Bailando," which means "dancing," Mora described the scene:

> *I will remember you dancing,*
> *Spinning round and round*
> *A young girl in Mexico . . .*
> *years later smiling into my eyes*
> *when I'd reach up to dance with you*
> *my dear aunt, who years later*
> *danced with my children,*
> *you white-haired but still young*
> *waltzing on your ninetieth birthday,*
> *more beautiful than the orchid*
> *pinned on your shoulder. . . .* (*Chants*, p. 51)

Two years after *A Birthday Basket for Tía* was published, Mora was invited to visit an elementary school in rural

Kentucky, not far from her home at the time, which was in Cincinnati, Ohio. Mora had been asked by teachers at the school to share her writing with the students and talk to them about how she plans and writes storybooks and poetry. After she spoke to the classes and ate lunch with the students in the school cafeteria, Mora took a tour of the school. During this time, several of the young students approached Mora and told her that they enjoyed reading *A Birthday Basket for Tía*.

Then, one girl presented Mora with a book that the students had written and fashioned on their own, titled *Birthday Baskets for Special People*. On each page, the students had drawn birthday baskets and filled them with gifts for special people in their lives. "Like Cecilia in my book, they had filled the baskets with objects the child and receiver enjoy together," Mora said. "The students had written their dedications on the backs of their drawings." (*A Latina in Kentucky*, p. 298) Although each student had dedicated a page in the book to the special person in his or her lives, the entire book was dedicated to Mora, who was touched:

> How privileged I felt as I drove back through the hills that afternoon to Cincinnati. I had been reminded of why I write for children, of their generosity, curiosity, and creativity. The drawings of baskets from those Kentucky youngsters are here for me on days when a writer's frustrations—rejection letters, letters of publication delays, no letters!—have me momentarily wondering why I spend my nontravel days here, alone, working. I turn the pages of their book, see their baskets filled with trucks, worms, dolls, lizards, baseballs, guitars. I read

AUNT LOBO

the dedications. One says, "To mom and dad: 1. Candy canes, I like to eat candy canes. 2. Books, I like to read books." (*A Latina in Kentucky*, p. 298)

Pat Mora (center) poses with her parents, Estela Delgado (left) and Raúl Antonio Mora (right), and one of her sisters, Cecilia. When Mora started writing, she used the stories of her parents' lives as the basis of some of her stories and poems.

2

A Writer Emerges

THE STONE HOUSE where Patricia Estella Mora grew up is located at 704 Mesita Street, in El Paso, Texas. Mora's father, Raúl Antonio Mora, had the house built for his bride, Estela Delgado. Estela had been hoping that Raúl would use his money for a fancy honeymoon in the Mexican resort towns of Monterrey or Guadalajara, but Raúl was immensely proud of their new house. Each day, while the construction crews worked on the house, Raúl would show up and kick the walls to make sure they were sturdy.

Mesita Street is located in a quiet neighborhood in El Paso, Texas. Pat Mora was born in El Paso on January 19, 1942. When she was a young girl, Pat and her sisters and brother played in the nearby desert and enjoyed catching tiny lizards that slithered across the sand. To the east, she could see the rocky Franklin Mountains rising high from the desert landscape. Later, when Mora became a poet and children's book writer, she would often find inspiration in the landscape and culture of the desert.

Sometimes, when Mora needed to be alone to think about her life and future, she would take a walk. She knew she could find comfort in the solitude of the vistas of the desert and mountains. She said, "Even as a teenager, when you're carrying around all this angst, when you came [in] here, you knew it was going to be quiet. It was a place for reflection. How can you not be shaped by these kinds of spaces?"[4]

Mora's parents also influenced her writing. She has based some of her stories and poems on the lives of Raúl and Estela Mora. Mora recalled her father's willingness to work hard and her "feisty, articulate" mother's devotion to reading and education.

"My father had a wonderful attitude toward life," Mora said. "He was never a bitter man. He liked work, and probably couldn't understand anybody who didn't. He had a knack for making the best of a difficult situation. A great sense of humor, a fantastic teaser. He had a very good heart. He always thought people were doing the best they could do."[5]

When he was seven years old, Raúl Mora started selling newspapers on El Paso street corners. By the age of 10, he was one of the most successful newsboys in El Paso, selling his papers to busy people as they hurried by, either on

A WRITER EMERGES

Pat Mora (right) poses with her sisters, Stella (center) and Cecilia (nicknamed Cissy). Pat and her sisters played in the nearby desert and enjoyed catching the tiny lizards that lived there.

their way to work in the morning or on their way home in the evening. As an adult, he held an important job in the circulation department of a local Spanish language newspaper. Even during the Depression, when many Americans were out of work and money was hard to come by, Raúl Mora was successful. He earned more than $100 a week, which was a princely sum that few Americans, much less a Latino American, could earn in the 1930s. Like many Latinos, he suffered from discrimination during that era but worked hard to find decent jobs. Raúl Mora later reminisced about those days, telling his daughter that, while others were forced to live on pennies, "I'm a rich man, honey. That's a lot of money then." (*House of Houses*, p. 89)

The story of Pat Mora's family in the United States actually began in 1915, when Mora's paternal grandparents, Lázaro and Natividad Mora, fled Mexico to escape the bloodshed of the Mexican Revolution. Before they left for the United States, the Moras had lived in the Mexican state of Chihuahua, where the notorious bandit Pancho Villa led raids against the government of the corrupt Mexican dictator Venustiano Carranza. Gunfights between bandits and government troops were common in Chihuahua, and her grandparents feared violence even as they fled north and crossed the Río Grande into Texas. The Moras and their three-year-old son, Raúl, settled in El Paso, Texas, a city just across the Río Grande from Juárez, Mexico.

Meanwhile, Eduardo and Amelia Delgado, also from Mexico, married in El Paso, where their daughter Estela was born. Estela was a bright student and dedicated reader, a trait she would pass on to her children. In high school, Estela won many speech contests and hoped to go to college to become a writer, but her family could not afford to send her to college. In 1934, at the age of 17, she met Raúl Mora on a blind date. They married five years later.

"My mother was a wonderful speaker," recalled Mora.

> She was the first in the family on her side to speak English. She defied the stereotypes. When she started school, she was the shining star, a true extrovert, though her parents were both very quiet. She wanted to be the one speaking in the auditorium. She was the one always raising her hand. She doesn't know how it happened. I think it amazes her.[6]

Raúl left the newspaper because of a problem with the new owners, and enrolled in a local business college, where he studied typing, shorthand, bookkeeping, and

A WRITER EMERGES 25

Estela Delgado's parents (Pat Mora's maternal grandparents), Eduardo and Amelia Delgado, are shown above in their wedding portrait. They married in El Paso, Texas, early in the twentieth century.

other skills he would need to go into business for himself. Soon, though, Raúl's money ran out and he was forced to drop out of college. He found a job where he fixed car batteries, but it was not a job he enjoyed. The batteries were filled with acid, which ate into Raúl's clothes and formed holes in his pants. Raúl was so embarrassed that he waited until dark before walking home, because he did not want his friends and neighbors to see him dressed in tattered clothes.

Raúl would not have that problem for long. In 1939, the year he married Estela, Raúl's eldest sister, Chole, approached a friend at Riggs Optical, an eyeglasses manufacturer in El Paso, and asked him to help Raúl find a job at the company. Chole's friend agreed, and Raúl was hired. He spent the next 10 years at Riggs Optical, where he learned the business. Finally, in 1949, Raúl left Riggs Optical to found his own company.

In the meantime, Raúl and Estela started their family. In addition to Patricia, they had two more daughters, Cecilia and Stella, and a son, Roy Antonio. All of the children helped out in the business. In fact, Mora recalled that *antiojos*, or "eyeglasses," was one of the first words she learned as a toddler. There were always tasks to do at the business. Mora said, "When we aren't in school or doing homework, my sisters and I go to the optical [company] and clean the desks or wash finished glasses, but there's always a reward, a stop at the Oasis Drive-In."[7]

INTEREST IN READING

The Moras enrolled their children in the local Catholic schools. Pat attended St. Patrick's School in El Paso, where nuns from the order known as the Sisters of Loretto taught the classes. The sisters were very influential in Pat's life, and she harbored ambitions to enter the order and become a nun and teacher herself well into her teenage years. In fact, she often played a game at home where she dressed in a black lace shawl and rearranged the dining room furniture into rows of pews. Then, Pat played at leading the class in the lessons she learned from the nuns at school. She even picked out the name she planned to use after entering the order: Sister Mary Jude, so she could honor Jude, the patron saint of the impossible.

Estela Mora made sure her children dedicated themselves to reading. Mora recalled that, no matter how busy her mother seemed to be, she would always make time to take the children to the library. "I'm a reader because of my mother," Mora said. "When she was little, she'd hide under the covers with a flashlight to finish her books. She always bought books for us and took us to the library until we were old enough to go by bus. I joined the summer reading clubs."[8]

One of Pat's favorite authors was Laura Ingalls Wilder, author of *Little House on the Prairie* and other books about pioneer life. Mora also read books featuring Nancy Drew, the fictional girl detective; Pollyanna, a plucky young heroine who always had a bright outlook when things grew darkest; and the Bobbsey Twins, two sets of fraternal twins who were the featured characters of many mystery and adventure books.

Pat also enjoyed reading nonfiction books about some of the leading figures in history, including Clara Barton, Davy Crockett, Amelia Earhart, Betsy Ross, William Penn, Dolly Madison, and Jim Bowie. "I have always been a reader, which is the best preparation for becoming a writer," Mora explained. "When I was in grade school in El Paso, Texas . . . I read comic books and mysteries and magazines and library books. I was soaking up language." (*My Own True Name*, p. 1)

Pat Mora poses at her family's celebration for her first communion. First communion is a Roman Catholic ceremony that takes place when a child receives the sacrament of the Eucharist for the first time, usually around the age of seven or eight.

A WRITER EMERGES

BILINGUAL HOME

In fact, Pat was soaking up two languages. The Mora house was bilingual, which means that the Moras spoke both English and Spanish. At home, Pat's grandmother and aunt spoke mostly Spanish, and her father enjoyed listening to the traditional Mexican music known as mariachi on the radio. Still, even though Mexico was just across the border, and El Paso had a large population of Latinos, there was little in the way of Mexican culture taught at school. "There were times when I wished that my Mexican heritage were a part of my school day," Mora said. "I wish that we had had books that had Spanish in them. And I wish that I had seen things about Mexican culture on the bulletin boards and in the library."[9] At times, though, Mora remembers that she found her Spanish-speaking relatives and her father's love for mariachi music to be embarrassing. She often wondered why they did not act more like "Americans."

Later, as a poet and children's book author, Mora would become an advocate for bilingual education in America and publish many of her stories and poems in both languages. She said, "One of the reasons that I write children's books is because I want Mexican culture and Mexican American culture to be a part of our schools and libraries."[10]

When Pat graduated from the eighth grade, her parents gave her a typewriter as a gift. Before this, Pat had never thought of becoming a writer, but she discovered how effortlessly the words seemed to pour from her fingers when she sat down in front of the typewriter. She started to write poetry at the typewriter. "I still remember how good the keys felt under my fingers, the way they feel now when

I work at my computer," Mora said. "When I was growing up, I never met or saw a writer, and don't think I considered being one until I was an adult. I was too busy planning to be a nun!"[11]

At school, Pat and the other students were required to memorize many poems. Although she recalled complaining about the task at the time, she eventually came to realize that memorizing a poem taught her a lot about how it was

Did you know...

Pat Mora was educated in Catholic schools and taught by nuns from the order of the Sisters of Loretto. She credits the Loretto sisters for teaching her to appreciate poetry and helping to hone her talent as a writer.

A Belgian Catholic priest named Charles Nerinckx, together with three pioneer women in Kentucky, founded the Sisters of Loretto in 1812. Their first school was a log cabin in the Kentucky woods, which they named "Little Loretto," after the shrine in Italy that honors the home of Jesus, Mary, and Joseph in Nazareth. Nerinckx and the sisters dedicated the order to the education of youth.

After the Mexican War, the United States gained vast amounts of territory in the Southwest. In 1852, Bishop Jean-Baptiste Lamy of Sante Fe, New Mexico, asked the Sisters of Loretto to establish Catholic schools throughout the Southwest. That November, the Loretto sisters opened their first school in Sante Fe. The sisters established the first Loretto school in Texas, St. Joseph's Academy, in San Elizario, near El Paso, in 1879. As Sister

A WRITER EMERGES

written, how the poet intended it to be interpreted, and how the poet preferred that it be recited. Mora recalled,

> I had many wonderful teachers who had us memorize poetry. Although, at the time, I probably grumbled and griped about it—it was helpful to me. Some of those poems I still remember. . . . In eighth grade we had to memorize a poem every week and recite it on Friday. But I always liked poetry and I

Mary Bernard Doyle described the school when she arrived in 1874:

> We were met in El Paso by two sisters in a canvassed-top spring wagon. The driver looked like he had never known soap, water, or a comb. Finally, we reached San Elizario after dark the same evening. When daylight dawned upon us, really my impressions were not very encouraging, as it seemed we had reached God's forsaken part of the world. . . . The church had no pews, a mud floor; the highways were full of ruts and holes.*

Loretto Academy, the high school that Mora attended, opened in 1923 with 143 students and 8 teachers. The school continues to educate students. Today, the sisters work with troubled El Paso youths, lead adult education classes, and perform other services for the people of El Paso.

* Quoted in "Sisters of Loretto Have Long Tradition in the Southwest," Borderlands, an El Paso Community College Local History Project. http://www.epcc.edu/nwlibrary/borderlands/19_loretto.htm.

Pat Mora poses in her cap and gown for her graduation from high school at the Loretto Academy. By the time she graduated, Mora had changed her mind about her future career: instead of wanting to be a nun, she aspired to become a doctor.

had lots of books in my house so I would just open them up and read all sorts of poetry.[12]

Mora has always believed that she owes a debt to the nuns of the Loretto order for helping to hone her talent as a writer. She dedicated her 1997 book of poetry, *Aunt Carmen's Book of Practical Saints*, to the Sisters of Loretto.

For high school, Pat enrolled in Loretto Academy, which was also taught by the Sisters of Loretto. She excelled there, but she still had given no thought to becoming a writer. Instead, Pat strongly considered entering medical school and studying to be a doctor. At the age of 17, Pat had seen *The Nun's Story*, a film that starred actress Audrey Hepburn as a young woman who gives up a life of wealth and leisure to become a nun and nurse in Africa. Pat decided that she did not want to be a nun or a nurse, but she felt that as a doctor she could use her talents to help people. "It was a time of those wonderful Audrey Hepburn movies about those missionary nuns who go out to save the world," Mora recalled. "I decided I would go out and save the world by being a doctor."[13]

In 1960, Pat graduated from Loretto Academy and enrolled in Texas Western College, which today is known as the University of Texas-El Paso. She entered college as a premed major, but after two years, she changed her mind and decided to become a teacher. She graduated from Texas Western in 1963 and soon found a job as an English and Spanish teacher in the El Paso schools. She also married her boyfriend, William H. Burnside Jr. The couple would have three children: Bill, Libby, and Cissy.

"NOW OR NEVER"

Many writers toil for years in obscurity, constantly sending out manuscripts to publishers only to receive cold rejection letters in return. Although many become frustrated and give up, that was not the case with Mora. She was very busy as a mother of three children. For the first part of her life, she had little time to write and, therefore, did not grow frustrated waiting for the publishing world to discover her talent.

In 1971, Mora joined the faculty of El Paso Community College, where she taught English part-time. Her students there, and later at the University of Texas–El Paso, were required to compose essays. Mora slowly came to the realization that her students were doing more writing than she was. In 1981, she transferred out of the English department and took a position as an assistant to the vice-president of the college. The hours spent in an office would be longer, and Mora would also have to leave classroom teaching, which she thoroughly enjoyed. Still, Mora believed that as a college administrator, her evenings and weekends would be freer to pursue writing. She said, "The seemingly endless stacks of essays to read and a growing desire to write finally convinced me to apply for a position that might require a long day, but allow evenings and weekends for my children and my writing."[14]

There would, in fact, be another dramatic change in her life that year: Mora and her husband, William, agreed to divorce. Nearly 40 years old, Mora realized that, if she intended to pursue a career as a writer, she would have to start right away. "When I went through my divorce and I realized I was edging toward 40, I said to myself, it's now or never. If you're not going to be serious about writing, it's never going to happen."[15]

SOURCE OF PRIDE

What should Mora write about? She soon concluded that she knew a great deal about the Latino experience in America, because she had been a part of that experience herself. She would therefore write about Latinos, as well as their struggles, their lives at home, and their culture. Mora discovered that, although she knew a lot about Mexican Americans, the El Paso schools had taught her very little about Mexicans and Mexico.

Mora began to read about Mexico and its history, and she was deeply affected by what she read. As she was drawn into the story of her people, Mora felt a fierce pride well up inside her. She recalled, "I experienced that not uncommon transformation experienced by many whose pasts have been ignored or diminished: I began to see Mexico, to see its people, hear its echoes, gaze up at its silent and silenced grandeur. My Mexicanness became a source of pride."[16]

In 1981, Mora's first poem to be published appeared in a Latino anthology of poetry for children. It was a good beginning, to be sure, and there was no denying that Mora was a talented writer. In 1983, she received the Award for Creative Writing from the National Association for Chicano Studies. A year later, her first book of poetry, *Chants*, was published; it included poems about the desert landscape around El Paso. Writing in the Latino literary journal *Revista Chicano-Riqueña,* editor Julián Olivares said, "Like the desert, Pat Mora speaks with muted tones, weaves incantations; she invests her poetic space with magical figures, yet from her loneliness come as well fear, resentment and despair. But she learns the peaceful solitude of the desert. From their dialogue, words become blossoms, fragile in desert rhythms."[17] In 1986, she followed *Chants* with *Borders,* a second book of poetry. Again, the critics praised the effort.

Meanwhile, both her personal and her professional life continued to undergo significant change. In 1984, Mora married her second husband, Vernon Scarborough, who was an archaeologist. She also became assistant to the university president, and she won an appointment as the director of the university's museum.

Mora continued to write, and in 1986, she was awarded a Kellogg National Leadership Fellowship to study foreign cultures, sponsored by the Kellogg Foundation. In 1989, Scarborough, who was an expert in the culture of the Maya Indians, accepted a teaching position at the University of Cincinnati in Ohio. Mora resigned her job at the university, and the couple moved to Cincinnati. Instead of looking for a new job, Mora decided to become a full-time writer and consultant. After she traveled extensively in Europe and Asia, Mora returned to the United States to write *Communion,* her third book of poetry. It included poems about her experiences traveling in New York City, as well as in France, Canada, Cuba, India, and Pakistan. Eventually, Mora and Scarborough returned to the Southwest, establishing a home in Santa Fe, New Mexico.

WRITING ABOUT TWO CULTURES

Communion was published in 1991. Soon, Mora conceived the idea of a book that centered on the life of her Aunt Lobo and the story of how her aunt tossed aside her cane to dance on her ninetieth birthday. It became *A Birthday Basket for Tía,* which was published in 1992.

Mora's elation over *A Birthday Basket for Tía* soon subsided. In 1993, just a few months after the book was published, her father, Raúl, died. Raúl Mora had retired from his optical company two years before. He soon grew depressed and developed dementia, a mental condition that made it difficult for him to remember familiar people and things. His final months were difficult ones, and it was a painful time for his family members, who were forced to watch his condition deteriorate. Later, Mora wrote about the final few days of her father's life:

> My father can no longer chew . . . baby food, puréed foods are spooned into his disinterested lips. He gets thinner. "I feel a burning. My stomach is on fire."
>
> Stella, his daughter/nurse, becomes his midwife, eases the father she loves out of this life with puddings she works down his throat, ice chips she places on his tongue, glycerin swabs she smoothes on his silent lips to keep them from cracking.
>
> Her six-year-old son says, "Mom, it's time for Papa to die." The boy comes and leans on his grandfather's body. "Papa, I came to say good-bye. Take care of yourself. Say hi to Baby Jesus for me. Look down and take care of me. I'll see you in heaven." My father squeezes his grandson's hand.
>
> The day before his body dies, his lips move with difficulty, but he whispers to his youngest daughter, Stella, "Take care of yourself, honey." (*House of Houses*, p. 113)

For Mora, the memories of her father, as well as the other members of her family, would live on. Indeed, the memories of her life growing up in El Paso would provide a tremendous inspiration for her as a poet and an author of books for children. When Mora was a young girl, she could look east across the Río Grande and see Juárez, Mexico. Back in the 1940s and 1950s, there were no electric lights in the outskirts of Juárez. At night, only the cooking fires were visible. Mora was very interested in the people of Juárez and the other towns on the Mexican side of the border. In the years after her father's death, she would write many poems and books exploring life along the border and what it meant to belong to the cultures of both countries.

In Spanish, the name El Paso means "the pass." The city earned its name because it is the point at which many Mexicans cross into the United States. The photograph above, from 1909, shows the international bridge into El Paso from the vantage point of Juárez, Mexico.

3

Living on the Border

IN SPANISH, *EL Paso* means "the Pass." The city was given that name because many Mexicans who traveled north regarded the city as the passageway into the United States. Indeed, students learn in school that European immigrants entered the United States through Ellis Island, and Asians entered through the Angel Island immigration station near San Francisco. They learn very little, however, about the harrowing journeys that Mexicans made north into Texas, New Mexico, California, and other southwestern states. Today, more than 25 million people of Mexican descent live in the United States. Whether they entered the country legally or illegally, many of those

Mexicans or their ancestors arrived in the United States by crossing the Río Grande.

"I've always been grateful living in a city where I could see Mexico, the country of my grandparents," Mora said.

> I could go back and forth to Mexico as I was growing up. When you live on the border you don't think anything of it. We would go over for dinner, or to a concert, or to buy bread. When I was growing up, we crossed back and forth by car or we walked without any trouble at all. My interest in borders, in all kinds of borders, I think comes from that experience.[18]

As someone who grew up on the Mexico-U.S. border, Mora has tried to be a part of two cultures. At home, most of her family members spoke English and Spanish, but her grandmother spoke only Spanish. Mora knows that there is more to being bicultural than simply learning two languages. In her book for children about her mother, *The Rainbow Tulip*, Mora tells the story of first-grader Estelita, who lives in a home where Spanish is spoken, but who must speak English at school, where she is called Stella:

> My father gives us an *abrazo*, a hug, and says, *"Buenos días, hijos."* My mother and father came to this country from Mexico. They don't speak English.
>
> My brothers and I speak English outside the house and Spanish inside the house. My father says, *"Hija*, this house is a piece of Mexico." (*The Rainbow Tulip*)

At school, the class is to take part in the upcoming May Day parade. The girls in Stella/Estelita's class are to march in the parade dressed as tulips. Estelita tells her Aunt Carmen, who will make the costume, to fashion a tulip dress of many colors. When May Day arrives, Estelita arrives at school with the most colorful costume in the class, and all the other girls are dressed in costumes of a single color. Although Estelita is embarrassed that her costume is unlike the others, she participates in the parade. During the parade, Estelita sees her mother, who is dressed in a black dress. She looks different from the other mothers, who are dressed fashionably and wear makeup. Estelita knows that her mother stands out from the others and, in fact, cannot talk to the other parents because she doesn't speak English.

Later, at home, Estelita's mother tells her she is proud of her and gives her a bowl of lime sherbet. Estelita says, "'It's hard to be different,'" says my mother. "'It's sweet and sour, like your sherbet.'" (*The Rainbow Tulip*)

LATINO CULTURE NEGLECTED

In *The Rainbow Tulip*, Mora based the character of Stella/Estelita on her mother, Estela Delgado. Even though El Paso had a large Latino population when Mora was young, as it does today, the schools did not teach Spanish or explore Mexican culture. Like many of her classmates, Mora came from a home where her family spoke both English and Spanish, but once she walked through the doorway of the school building, she spoke only English. According to Mora, Latino schoolchildren learned nothing about the language that their parents and grandparents spoke at home, and they learned nothing about the culture of their ancestors. Said Mora,

> It's interesting to me that though I lived in a very bilingual community, Spanish was never mentioned at school. Many of my friends also came from bilingual homes—or, certainly from homes where Spanish was spoken. And I visited those homes, just as I visited the homes of my monolingual English friends; but Spanish and being of Mexican descent and being

Pat Mora (right) poses with her mother, Estela, and sister Cissy. Mora based the character of Stella/Estelita in the story **The Rainbow Tulip** *on her mother.*

part of the border experience was never part of my educational experience.[19]

Mora did not come to realize that her Latina culture and language were neglected in school until many years later. When she started her career as a writer, she discovered that there were few books on school library shelves that directly addressed the Latino experience in America, particularly the life of young Latino school students. "I realized that part

Did you know...

Pat Mora prefers to be described as a Latina or Chicana, the feminine forms of Latino and Chicano. She said she prefers those terms over Hispanic, which is used routinely to describe people with some Spanish heritage. She says, "I'm very comfortable if people say 'Chicana, Latina, Mexican American,'" she said. "I don't have any trouble with those. 'Hispanic' I have a little more problem with."*

Mora explained that "Hispanic" is a word that was commonly used in Europe as a description for people of Spanish ancestry, so the word more accurately describes people from Spain than people from Mexico, whose heritage is both Spanish and Indian.

"To be more proud of the Spanish side than of the indigenous side bothers me a lot," she said.**

Mora said she accepts Chicano and Chicana, which are terms applied specifically to Mexican Americans, but she prefers Latino and Latina because those terms describe all people of Spanish and native heritages, including Mexicans, Cubans, Puerto Ricans, and South and Central Americans.

---

* Quoted in Elisabeth Mermann-Jozwiak and Nancy Sullivan, "Interview with Pat Mora," *Melus* Vol. 28, No. 2 (Summer 2003): p. 139.

** Ibid.

of my life—a big part of my life—had never totally been welcomed in my educational experience," Mora said. "So, I was a good student. I loved school. I loved reading. And to some extent, I never noticed that part of what I was, was missing at school."[20]

In 2005, the U.S. Census Bureau's American Community Survey reported that Latinos had surpassed African Americans as the nation's largest minority group: 14.5 percent of the American population is Latino, and 12 percent of the population is black. Despite the growing Latino population of the United States, Mora said that only 2 percent of the books written for young readers are by Latinos or about Latinos.

The shortage of literature for young Latinos is largely what drives Mora to write storybooks for elementary school students, as well as for beginning readers. She said, "I write, in part, because Hispanic perspectives need to be a part of our literary heritage; I want to be part of that validation process."[21]

TWO CULTURES

Mora's poetry has also explored the issues of living on the border of two cultures. Certainly, her book of poems called *Borders* was devoted to the subject. She has also explored the clash of the Latino and non-Latino cultures in other poems. "Legal Alien," which was published in *Chants*, illustrates how many Mexican Americans do not know where to fit in:

> . . . *able to sit in a paneled office*
> *Drafting memos in smooth English,*
> *able to order in a fluent Spanish*
> *at a Mexican restaurant,*
> *American but hyphenated,*

> *viewed by Anglos as perhaps exotic,*
> *perhaps inferior, definitely different,*
> *their eyes say, "You may speak*
> *Spanish but you're not like me"*
> *an American to Mexicans*
> *a Mexican to Americans . . .* (*Chants*, p. 2)

Mora often wonders how her life would have been different if she had grown up on the Mexican side of the border. Certainly, she is aware of the poverty under which many Mexicans live and how, just a few hundred feet away, many Americans live in affluence and prosperity. "On the campus at which I went to school and where I worked, you actually look out at these very poor *colonias* on the other side of the Río Grande," Mora recalled. "I've always had that sense that I could have been born on the other side. So borders interest me."[22]

"Fences," one of Mora's poems in *Communion*, illustrates the different lifestyles led by the people who visit Mexico and some of the people who live in Mexico. The poem relates the experience of a family that works in a Mexican resort hotel. The mother cleans the hotel rooms, and a son works on the beach, smoothing the footprints so the American tourists can step onto fresh sand each morning. When a daughter runs across the beach, her mother scolds her, saying, "No. No. It's their beach. It's their beach." (*Authors in Depth*, p. 44) The beach should belong to the Mexican people, but in the poem, the poor Mexicans must maintain the sand in fine condition for the wealthy Americans who come south to enjoy the Mexican resort community.

Mora also addresses the assimilation of Mexicans into American society: She writes about the many young Latinos who strive to fit into American society, which often causes them to neglect the language and culture of their ancestors. In her poem "Immigrants," she wrote that newly arrived families,

> *Wrap their babies in the American flag*
> *feed them mashed hot dogs and apple pie*
> *name them Bill and Daisy*
> *buy them blonde dolls that blink blue*
> *eyes or a football and tiny cleats.* (*Borders*, p. 15)

Mora said that her own experience growing up in El Paso inspired her to write that poem. When Mora became an adult and started to study Mexico and its culture, she realized how much she did not know about the country of her ancestors. Mora described the change in her attitude:

> My Mexicanness became a source of pride. I had grown up in an environment that did not value, and often hated, my cultural heritage. Those in positions of power, the audible voices of political, educational, cultural, and economic leaders tried, some still try, to ignore or suppress—dark skin, the Spanish language, expressiveness. I, like so many dwellers in that Southwestern desert, grew up ambivalent. Being "American" was and is given great importance. (*Nepantla*, p. 41)

PASSIONATE ABOUT IMMIGRATION

In recent years, few issues have divided Americans more than illegal immigration. Some political leaders and others complain that illegal immigrants tax America's ability to provide social services such as housing and health care, since many illegal immigrants are poor and cannot provide for themselves. Critics charge that many illegal immigrants cannot find jobs and turn to crime. When illegal immigrants do find jobs, many fear that they take them away from citizens and other legal residents of the United States. In addition, some people express concern about security and worry that immigrants may bring weapons into the country. Moreover, some worry that people who enter the United States illegally might use those weapons in terror attacks.

Illegal immigration has been the subject of intense debate in the U.S. Congress, as well as many state legislatures throughout the country. In 2006, the U.S. Department of Homeland Security reported that the number of illegal immigrants living in the United States had reached 11 million. Many of them come from Latin American countries and, in particular, from Mexico. According to the Department of Homeland Security, some 260,000 illegal immigrants from Mexico entered the United States between 2000 and 2005, which means that more than 50,000 illegal immigrants from Mexico enter the United States each year, or nearly 1,000 immigrants each week.

Most of those immigrants make dangerous treks across open desert, hoping to evade U.S. Border Patrol agents. In 2006, to help stem the flow of illegal immigrants, Congress approved the expenditure of billions of dollars to erect a 700-mile (1,126-kilometer) fence that would separate Mexico from parts of California, Arizona, New Mexico, and Texas.

Mora uses her poetry to address the issue of illegal immigration, writing about the issue from the perspective of people living on both sides of the border. Indeed, her poetry has told the story of the immigrants who seek to enter the United States and the Americans who want to keep them out. Mora called one poem from 1995 "La Migra," which is a term Mexicans use for the U.S. Border Patrol. In it, she expresses the viewpoint of a border-patrol agent:

> *I get the badge and the sunglasses.*
> *You can hide and run,*
> *but you can't get away*

because I have a jeep.
Oh, and a gun. (*Agua Santa/Holy Water*, p. 104)

In the same poem, Mora addresses the issue from the viewpoint of the immigrant:

Your jeep has a flat,
and you have been spotted by the sun.
I know this desert,
where to rest,
where to drink. (*Agua Santa/Holy Water*, p. 104)

Mora is very passionate about immigration, and believes that Mexicans who try to enter the country illegally are generally not a threat to the safety of Americans. She explained that:

The United States is a country of immigrants, and I think that it's easy for people to forget that. When I talk to students, when I visit schools, I talk to them about some of my sources of inspiration and I tell them that one of my sources is family. I'm very interested in having them think about their families. One of the suggestions I make is that they try to think back or learn about who were the people in their family who came to this country. And how did they come? Why did they come? I feel that ill will is generated through fear, and it serves no one well.[23]

"I AM THE RAINBOW TULIP"

Clearly, Mora believes that immigrants, particularly illegal immigrants, face hostility in the United States. They are often the victims of discrimination, she said. "I do feel that it is easy to target people who have darker skin, who don't have big bank accounts, and sometimes people generalize about a group, and so they will say 'this is what Latinos are like' when within every group, we're going to see a lot of diversity and a lot of variety."[24]

Even more important, discrimination also serves to rob many Latino young people of their heritage. According to Mora, young Latinos do not want to become victims of racial prejudice, so some try to act more like non-Latino Americans and less like Latino Americans. "Sometimes Latino students don't want to speak Spanish and don't want to claim their heritage because they see so many negative images about people who are like them," she said. "That always makes me sad and it makes Latino parents very sad."[25]

Mora hopes that her work has helped her Latino readers appreciate their cultural heritage. She believes that her children's books have been particularly effective in teaching Latino culture because they are written for very young readers who have the opportunity to learn about Latino culture as children.

In addition to the Latino audience, Mora believes that her books and poetry, like *The Rainbow Tulip*, can also reach Euro-Americans, Asian Americans, African Americans, and others. A school in Denver, Colorado, proved that Mora's books do reach other cultures. When she visited this school and spoke to members of a class who had just read *The Rainbow Tulip*, Mora said,

> I told the students that the statistics say one in every five children in the United States comes from a home in which a language other than English is spoken—one in five. The good part of the story is that in this school in Colorado, a young man stood up and said, "I am the only Polish student. I am the rainbow tulip." Well, that's the kind of story that makes an author really smile.[26]

Pat Mora posed for this photograph in 1963. She graduated from college at Texas Western that year and also married her then-boyfriend, William H. Burnside Jr. Shortly after graduating, Mora found a job as a teacher of both Spanish and English.

4

The Writer Is a Gardener

IN 1966, LONG before Pat Mora had established herself as a poet and an author, she conceived the idea for a children's book written in rhymes. She sent a book proposal to the Hallmark greeting card company, which also published children's literature. To her surprise, Hallmark bought the rights to the book, and the company paid her a fee of $100. Hallmark said in its letter to Mora that the company was not sure whether it would publish the story, but it wanted to secure the rights in case it decided to produce the book.

Mora regarded the $100 check as a triumph, and she believed it would only be a matter of time before Hallmark published the manuscript. In the meantime, Mora developed many ideas for stories and soon started pitching them to publishers. "Since nothing succeeds like success, I submitted 15 ideas for children's books to other publishers, and received all kinds of letters of rejection."[27]

In fact, Hallmark eventually decided not to publish Mora's book. None of the other publishers had much interest in her work, and it would be another 15 years before Mora produced a piece of writing that was actually published.

Rejection is a big part of a writer's life and, like most authors, Mora was forced to endure many letters of rejection on her road to a writing career. Still, she persevered and eventually convinced a publisher that her work merited publication. Mora advises new writers to "be prepared for rejection. Editors receive thousands of unsolicited manuscripts. Have I ever gotten used to the rejection? No."[28]

DEAR FELLOW WRITER

Mora enjoys helping new writers find their voices. The introduction to her 2000 book of poetry for teenagers, *My Own True Name*, was titled "Dear Fellow Writer." In the essay, Mora spoke about what motivates her to write, explaining that,

> Writing is my way of knowing myself, of hearing myself, of discovering what is important to me and what makes me sad, what makes me different, what makes me *me*—of discovering my own true name. And writing makes me less lonely. I have all these words in English and Spanish, whispering or sometimes shouting at me, just waiting for me to put them to work, to combine them so that they leap over mountains on small

THE WRITER IS A GARDENER

hooves or slip down to the sandy bottom of the silent sea. (*My Own True Name*, p. 2)

Of course, the first hurdle that Mora or any writer must cross is finding an idea and developing it into a story or a poem. For the most part, Mora relies on her memories, story ideas, and senses to provide her with inspiration. Her eyes see the images, and her ears hear the conversations of people or the sounds around her, whether they are in the city, the country, or the desert, which is a favorite topic. Mora talks about how this can happen anywhere:

> Writers are sometimes like insects because we have to have our antennae up. We have to be looking and listening for good ideas. And everything that happens to you in life can be a good idea for a book. I could be at a restaurant and get a good idea for a book. I could be at a museum. I can get ideas anywhere. Sometimes, when I'm walking along on the street and listening to people talk I get an idea. And then when I go back to my office I write a little bit more about it.[29]

Sometimes, the idea may come to Mora simply when she looks outside. Some of Mora's stories and poems are about flowers, birds, and other animals she can see from the windows of her home. She also draws on personal experiences from her childhood and has found inspiration in the lives of her family members. Mora keeps many photographs of her family members around her house. At times, those photos have provided some inspiration for another creative endeavor.

Although Mora used the experience of living with her aunt Lobo to write *A Birthday Basket for Tía,* she based the character of the little girl in the story on her own daughter, Cecilia. Since her daughter loves cats, Mora decided to create the character of Chica, the cat. Remembering shopping with her two children at a Mexican market in Juárez, Mora wrote *Unos Dos Tres/One, Two, Three* to help beginning readers learn how to count.

Mora spends many weeks a year traveling and speaking to students, teachers, and librarians across the country, and she often draws inspiration from the new sights and sounds she experiences on these trips. She recalled a time that she visited a new city, wandered into a Mexican bakery, and decided to write "Mexican Magician," a poem that described the activities of the bakers.

Writing, Mora believes, is a lot like tilling a garden. She explained, "I have been comparing the blank page to a new flowerbed, and talking about how writers come to that space with faith and hope. We have a vision of what we would like it to be. . . .We have to be stubborn and persistent. But it is the spirit of expectation that brings us back to the page."[30]

FIRST DRAFT IN LONGHAND

Mora seldom works on a single story or poem at a time; instead, she prefers to juggle many projects. She may be making the final changes on one manuscript, rewriting another manuscript after receiving comments from the editor, and submitting a proposal to a publisher on a third manuscript.

To begin a new story or poem, Mora tries to start working in the morning and finds a quiet place to sit. Mora explained that she finds a lot of inspiration in the dazzling scenery of the desert and sometimes writes outside. "The yard is, of course, a wonderful place to begin writing," she said. "My dream place to work is outside in the Southwest or where I can see the Southwest sky and mountains and desert. I've

THE WRITER IS A GARDENER

Pat Mora (left) signs books for young readers at a California library in 1994. Mora likes to encourage both young readers and young writers. She often points would-be poets to her poem "An Ode to Pizza," to demonstrate how poetry can be written about even the simplest of topics.

written a great deal, and will probably continue to explore, why my home landscape is so powerful for me."[31]

Typically, Mora writes at least part of the initial draft in longhand. Then, as the story or poem begins to take form, she moves to her desk and computer, where she finishes the draft. She often revises a manuscript many times before it is ready for submission to the editor.

Many of Mora's stories and poems are about Latinos and the deserts of the American Southwest, which are topics that have inspired her since she started writing. She urges all writers to study the subjects on which they choose to write. Indeed, even after many years of writing, Mora still takes time to research her topics. "I ask a lot of questions," she said. "That's one thing a good writer has to do. Don't be embarrassed to ask questions."[32]

In Mora's picture book titled *Listen to the Desert: Oye al Desierto,* she described the sounds of the animals of the desert. To research the story, she listened carefully to the desert sounds around her. "You can hear all these sounds in the desert," she said. "You can hear the wind and the doves and if it had rained maybe I'd hear some frogs."[33] In the book, she was able to duplicate the sounds for her readers by using words that mimicked the voices of animals.

Mora makes many notes about things she sees and hears. Later, those notes may be turned into a story or a poem. "One of the things that writers do is they write themselves a lot of notes, and then they don't lose those good ideas,"[34] she said.

According to Mora, writers must also learn to love the language in which they choose to write. They must constantly learn new words and new ways to use the words they know. It is particularly important for poets to listen

THE WRITER IS A GARDENER

to how words sound, and this can help writers train themselves to look at the world from a different perspective. She explained that,

> Sometimes, the names of plants can be funny. One of the reasons I like cactuses is they have very funny names—like *burro's tail*. Oh! The tail of a donkey. Or, there's a green cactus that looks like a brain. I wonder what it is thinking? One of my favorites is called the Old Man Cactus—the cactus is covered in long white hair and looks like a little old man. Sometimes I take pictures, too, so when I go back to my office I can have those pictures to remind me of what I saw.[35]

FAITH IN THE PROCESS

Mora cautions many new writers of children's literature and other genres to remember that the writer and publisher often have very different goals. The goal of a writer is, of course, to write a good story or poem. The goal of the publisher is to find a piece of writing that he or she can sell in the form of a book. Mora said that many new writers are often disappointed when they find a publisher who is willing to publish their work, but the editor requests changes. The publisher wants to make the story more marketable to book buyers, and Mora urges writers to learn to compromise on the editor's suggestions.

In addition to the writer and editor, many other people are involved in the production of a book: the publisher, art director, the marketing staff, and the illustrator if it is a storybook. Typically, the writer has little or no input in selecting the illustrator for the story. In fact, Mora said, she has written more than 25 storybooks and has met very few of the artists who have provided the illustrations for them. Although Mora is always curious because she never knows

Did you know...

One of Pat Mora's most unusual poems is "An Ode to Pizza." It can be found in her 2000 book, *My Own True Name: New and Selected Poems for Young Adults*. Mora salutes "the bubbling rumors of tomatoes, the gossip of basil and bay leaves."* Later in the poem, Mora uses 17 words for cheese, each in a different language, including Spanish, English, Japanese, Vietnamese, and Romanian.

Mora said that, when young people ask her whether they can also write poetry, she often suggests they read "An Ode to Pizza." This helps them see how a writer can select a very common subject, such as a food that nearly everyone has tasted, and turn it into a subject for a poem. She explained,

> One of my hopes as a writer is that when young people read my work, they feel, "I'd like to try that—I'd like to try writing an ode to pizza. I'd like to try writing an original poem." That's when I feel I have done my best work because I love writing, and I want my readers to feel the same way. I want them to feel that they can write something good, and that they don't have to be like me in any way. A young writer just has to be someone who likes to play with words.**

* Pat Mora, *My Own True Name: New and Selected Poems for Young Adults*. Houston, Tex.: Piñata Books, 2000, p. 13.

** Interview with Pat Mora by Hal Marcovitz, October 25, 2006.

how an illustrator will choose to interpret her work, Mora said she has learned to accept the notion that producing a book for children is a collaborative process. This means that everyone involved must learn to cooperate and work as a team, so whenever she works with a new illustrator, Mora trusts the illustrator's judgment. She said,

> People say to me, "But how could you turn over a story you love to someone else?" But I believe that so much of writing involves developing faith in the process. You may not be always totally happy, but at the deepest level you have to hope the illustrator will bring to the book even more than the writer ever imagined.[36]

TIPS FOR NEW WRITERS

Mora has developed a series of tips for new writers. To begin with, she believes all writers must be good readers. In her essay "Dear Fellow Writer," she wrote, "Some of us like mysteries and some of us like memoirs, but writers are readers. We're curious to see what others are doing with words, but—what is more important—we like what happens to us when we open a book, how we journey into the pages." (*My Own True Name*, p. 2)

Of course, just as writers should be readers, they should also be writers. Mora urges all new writers to make time for themselves to write whatever genre they choose: short stories, poetry, or essays. In addition, Mora believes all writers should write about a subject they enjoy and care about. In her case, she said, writing about her Mexican heritage and the desert "was like opening a treasure chest."[37] She added, "When I talk to teachers, and when I talk to librarians, and when I talk to students, I say the trick is how we bring everything that we are to the page—everything. So that if a student happens to love science and love bugs, I always say to him that was always something you could write about, because you were excited about it."[38]

Mora's advice for writing children's books is listed on her personal Web site (www.patmora.com.). Some of her suggestions to writers include:

> **Love your work.** Mora writes that writers should "care about the process of writing" and, if they choose to write for young readers, "consider it an honor to write for children." She also cautions that "having a book published probably won't change your life, but being commited to writing and children can change your life and the lives of your readers."
>
> **Read picture books, both old and new.** Visit bookstores and libraries; talk to librarians and booksellers to find out the type of books young readers enjoy the most.
>
> **Take notes.** Find a place to keep them until you are ready to craft a story or a poem.
>
> **Join writers' groups and enroll in writing workshops.** Many libraries, schools, universities, and bookstores often sponsor writers' clubs or workshops.
>
> **Read books on creativity.** Mora suggests reading books such as *Art and Fear* by David Bayles and Ted Orland; *The Artist's Way* by Julia Cameron; *Writing Down the Bones* by Natalie Goldberg; and *Bird by Bird* by Anne Lamott.
>
> **Learn how to revise your work.** Mora calls this an "essential habit."
>
> **Learn about the publishing industry.** Before submitting your work, it may be helpful to research publishers to find out what type of stories they prefer. Most publishers maintain Web sites where they post their guidelines

for authors. Mora explains, "Know that publishing is a business. Wonderful books get published; wonderful manuscripts don't. A publisher has to believe that a manuscript will sell when it competes with 5,000 other books."[39]

- **Show your work to family members and friends**. Mora writes that "this will give you and others pleasure and will encourage you to write more."
- **Be prepared for rejection**. Mora admits that it is still difficult to accept rejection, even 40 years after Hallmark ultimately decided it did not want to publish her first children's book. Although Mora is a very successful author of children's and adult's books, she still gets rejection letters from time to time. Nevertheless, when one does arrive in the mail, Mora said, she never tosses away the manuscript. She looks it over to see whether she can rewrite. "I'm terribly disappointed," she said. "Eventually, I dust myself off and revise and resubmit."[40]

Pat Mora poses in her beloved New Mexico for this 1996 photograph. For her writing, Mora often draws on the landscapes and cultures that characterize the American Southwest.

5

The Making of a Poet

MORA DECIDED TO write a poem about how young people are often faced with difficult tasks, and some of them may question their own skills, trying to convince themselves that they cannot succeed. Using the Spanish word *víbora* for "snake," Mora compared the doubts and questions that plague young people to the flies that buzz around the head of a snake. In the poem "Old Snake," she wrote,

> *Old Snake knows.*
> *Sometimes you feel*
> *you just can't breathe*

in your own tight skin.
Old Vibora says, "Leave
those doubts and hurts
buzzing like flies in your ear.
When you feel your frowns,
like me wriggle free
from I can't, I can't.
Leave those gray words
to dry in the sand
and dare to show
your brave self,
your bright true colors. (*This Big Sky*)

Here, Mora's use of the image of a snake and flies in her poem is known as a metaphor. The poet or writer uses words that appear to have no direct application to the subject that is discussed in the text, but the images are symbols for what he or she is truly talking about. Metaphors are very common in poetry, as well as in other forms of literature. Mora explains that:

> The old snake says, "Leave those doubts and hurts buzzing like flies in your ear." Everybody knows what it's like to have one of those pesky flies buzzing about you. The poem is about how sometimes we feel we can't do something, and those words "I can't . . . I can't" are like flies buzzing in our ears. When I talk to students, they all have felt "I can't . . . I can't." . . . "I can't learn to ride a bike" or "I can't solve the math problem" or whatever. I want them to think about those negative words as just like those flies you can just brush away and move on.[41]

VAGUE MEANINGS

Mora is renowned as much for her poetry as for her books for young readers. Indeed, Mora has written poetry on many levels. She wrote her first three books of poetry, *Chants, Borders,* and *Communion,* for adult readers. She has also written poetry for teens, including an anthology titled *My One True Name: New and Selected Poems for Young Adults.* Books of poems for younger readers, such as *Confetti: Poems for Children* and *This Big Sky,* which includes the poem "Old Snake," are also well known.

Picture books, as well as books in chapter form, are generally written in prose. Prose uses words that have a concrete meaning and are to be taken at face value by readers. The story is written using common grammatical conventions so the reader may follow the action and draw the conclusions the writer intends. In poetry, however, the writer is freer to explore other literary styles and is not locked into the usual rules regarding paragraphs, sentence structure, capitalization, or punctuation. Poets sometimes write in rhymes, but a lot of poetry is unrhymed.

Of course, metaphors are very important in poetry, particularly in the poems that Mora writes, as she explained:

> Many times, when I sit down to write, I am not constantly thinking, "I need a metaphor in this line." I don't think I've ever had that conscious thought. Writers tend to be people who read, so if you spend quite a bit of your life, as I have, reading, there are things that you do almost automatically, because you know that you have enjoyed it as a reader. The idea of giving an example—a metaphor—is a way of helping my reader see what I am seeing.[42]

Sometimes, though, Mora and other poets use metaphors that have vague meanings. Because of this, different readers will draw different conclusions about what they truly mean. For example, in the poem "Secrets," Mora wrote,

> *His feet could read mountains,*
> *dark, hard, bare feet, beating*
> *a rhythm in the canyons,*
> *season by season, feeling paths*
> *no one else saw . . .* (*Borders*, p. 86)

In this case, one of the metaphors that Mora uses is "read." Obviously, feet cannot read, but Mora suggested that the man had walked over the same mountain paths so often that his feet knew the trail as well as his eyes did. Perhaps Mora had another idea in mind. After all, in the next two lines she wrote that the man's feet beat rhythms, as though they are drumsticks. She may have implied that a lone man walking along a trail adds to the sounds, or the music, of the wilderness.

Indeed, there are a lot of meanings that can be drawn from those few lines of poetry. In many poems, readers are challenged to come up with the answers to the questions posed by the poets. For Mora's part, she encourages her readers to draw their own conclusions. She said,

> I try not to have a message when I start out. I really do. If I have a message then I say to myself, 'That's great, but that's not a poem.' I like to begin with an idea, a line, an image, and see where it goes. But I am stubborn enough that a lot of my deep feelings are obviously going to come in, because of the way I see the world.[43]

DESCRIPTIVE LANGUAGE

When writing poetry, Mora tries to use very descriptive words. For her poem "Tall Walking Woman" in *This Big Sky*, she wanted to describe the color of the blouse worn by a Native American woman. The blouse was red, but there can be a lot of variations on the color red, running the spectrum from pink to purple. In the poem, Mora used words to describe the exact shade of red she had in mind. "I say, 'Her blouse is the red of plump summer plums.' If I hadn't said 'plump summer plums,' you might not even notice the red, or the red that you saw might not be the red that I'm trying to describe," said Mora. "But by using "plump summer plums," I'm hoping that what you see is closer to what I want you to see."[44]

A well-written poem, according to Mora, helps the reader look below the surface to probe other meanings the writer had in mind. "I probably am trying to intrigue the reader—that's the word I might use," she explained. "I subscribe to the notion that the poem itself should be an experience. It's not just words on the page that someone is going to be tested on. No one writes poetry for that reason. So it is creating an experience that allows the reader to feel what I feel, to hear what I hear, to see what I see."[45]

Another factor that separates poetry from prose is the length. Most poems are not longer than a page or so, and they are often quite short. There are exceptions, of course; the poets of ancient Greece and medieval Europe wrote poems that were often dozens or even hundreds of pages in length. Still, Mora believes that, since the average contemporary poem is typically brief, the poet's task is often quite different from the prose writer's. The prose writer can take several pages to convey an idea, but the poet must do the same job in a handful of lines. Mora explained, "I consider poetry the ultimate challenge because you're trying to do so much with fewer words. I love the challenge of it."

Poetry and prose may differ in length, use of language, grammar, punctuation, and metaphors. One thing the two genres may have in common is that they can both be used to tell a story. A good example of a poem that tells a story is "Elena," which describes the plight of a Latina woman who is working very hard to make a living in the United States. Her children, who are students in high school, speak English very well, but Elena struggles with her new language. Mora said she was inspired to write "Elena" after hearing about the woman who was working in a nursing home in California. In the poem, Mora was able to give a very complete picture of Elena, even though the poem is no more than 22 lines. Even this short excerpt is very descriptive:

> *. . . I'm forty,*
> *embarrassed at the laughter of my children,*
> *the grocer, the mailman. Sometimes I take*
> *my English book and lock myself in the bathroom,*
> *say the thick words softly,*
> *for if I stop trying, I will be deaf*
> *when my children need my help.* (Chants, p. 50)

According to Mora, it has taken her as little as a few minutes to write drafts for some poems, but others have taken much longer. After writing a poem, Mora always reads it aloud to herself. Then, she must revise it:

I put it aside for awhile and I might come back to it in an hour or two and begin to cross out a word, or a slew of words. Maybe by the next day I may reorder; maybe the first part goes and the whole poem begins to move up. I think that the whole process is a very interesting one to the writer, though maybe not exactly what you call headline material. If we are thinking about students, if they're serious about being writers, whatever job they are going into, they should test themselves by seeing if they enjoy the revision process. It's just like being a cook: if you like the dessert when it's finished but you really didn't enjoy putting it together very much, you're not going to be one of those people who says, "I just love to cook."[47]

POETS WHO INSPIRE

Mora believes all poets should read poetry written by others, and she admires the work of Mary Oliver and Lucille Clifton, two contemporary American poets. Oliver is a winner of a Pulitzer Prize and a National Book Award, two of America's most prestigious awards for literature and poetry. "She writes what I think are incredible poems about the natural world," said Mora. "She is writing about the world in New England, and I am writing about a very different landscape in the Southwest, but the careful attention that she gives to every word is a very important influence to me."[48]

Like Mora, Lucille Clifton writes poetry and storybooks for children. An African American woman, Clifton displays a fierce pride in her poems. Clifton is also a staunch advocate for the rights of women. "She is a bold example to me of a poet who has used her own stories and her pride in being black as a deep well of ideas for her work,"[49] said Mora.

As for Latino poets, Mora admires the work of Federico García Lorca, the Spanish poet and playwright who was murdered in 1938 during the Spanish Civil War. García Lorca opposed the rise of fascism in Spain under the dictator Francisco Franco. Franco, who eventually ruled Spain for nearly four decades, is reputed to have ordered García Lorca's assassination. García Lorca's poetry is renowned for its strong use of the Spanish language and colorful metaphors. "He is also a playwright, but it is his poetry and the music of his poetry that I feel I can learn from,"[50] said Mora.

A POET FOR PRESIDENT

Another poet who Mora says has influenced her work is Pablo Neruda, a Chilean who won the Nobel Prize for Literature in 1971. The Nobel Prize is the most prestigious award for literature in the world. Neruda, who died in 1973, wrote poetry about war-torn nations: Spain, where he fought in the Spanish Civil War in the 1930s, and Chile, where he became a hunted man for opposing the government of President González Videla.

Mora especially admires Neruda because he was an activist poet, who was involved in political causes and then expressed himself through poetry. In Mora's opinion, many poets suffer from the impression that they live in a world apart from others: They do not toil at regular jobs, or they are indifferent to the problems of ordinary people. According to Mora, Latino poets like García Lorca and Neruda did get involved in political events and used their experiences to inform their readers of the oppressions suffered by ordinary people. Mora explains,

> I think, particularly in this country, people associate writers, especially poets, with people who are not connected to the real world. Latin America has such a different history for its writers. It was not unusual for a writer to also be a diplomat or very involved in speaking out in the country. There is, for example, the poet and essay writer Gabriela Mistral, who is the only Latin American woman who has won a Nobel Prize. Now when I read up on her, I am just so impressed because she was always speaking out for children and their

Did you know...

The work of Nobel Prize winner Pablo Neruda has had an enormous influence on Pat Mora's own poetry. A Chilean, Neruda was a statesman as well as a poet. He was born Neftalí Ricardo Reyes Basoalto in 1904, but he took the name Pablo Neruda to honor the Czech poet Jan Neruda, whose work he admired.

By the 1930s, Pablo Neruda was already a published poet when he accepted a position as a traveling emissary for the Chilean government. As he arrived in Spain, it was falling into civil war, and he became a sympathizer of the Republican movement, which was backed by socialists and communists. When agents of dictator Francisco Franco murdered Neruda's friend, poet and playwright Federico García Lorca, Neruda joined the Republicans.

Although Neruda's government soon recalled him to Chile, the poems he wrote during this period strongly supported the Republican cause and were circulated on the front lines during the conflict. Following the defeat of the Republicans by Franco, Neruda joined the Communist Party in Chile and continued to write politically volatile poetry.

Neruda's support for striking miners angered the government of Chilean President González Videla and made him a hunted man. Although he managed to escape from Chile in 1949, he was permitted to return in 1952. Neruda was awarded the Nobel Prize for Literature in 1971, two years before his death.

PAT MORA

Pablo Neruda is shown in a photograph from 1971. Neruda was one of Chile's most famous poets—a source of inspiration to many, including Pat Mora. Mora especially admired him because he was an activist as well as a poet, who was involved in important causes and used his poetry to communicate those causes to the public.

welfare, and really supporting women wherever she spoke around the world.

She represented her country—she was also Chilean—at many international conferences. She was a diplomat. I did an essay once for adults called "A Poet for President"—and played with that idea, how I think in the United States, people would think, "How can a poet possibly be a president? Poets are people who don't understand the facts."

It's an interesting question. Could a poet be president? My guess is that people would smile. Why is that? What is our image of people who are presidents, and what is our image of people who are poets? But I like the combination.[51]

A MUSICAL SURPRISE

Just as Mora has urged young people to become writers of children's books and other works in prose, she has also encouraged them to try to write poetry. After all, poetry was the first genre of writing in which Mora worked. As an eighth-grade student in El Paso, she wrote poetry on the typewriter her parents gave her for an eighth-grade graduation gift.

Mora encourages all writers to write poetry. She said,

> Writing poetry improves all writing. It is an ultimate challenge. It makes you conscious of the weight and sound of every word. Poetry is one of my sources of delight; it provides avenues for learning about the human heart including my own. Poetry is words woven together to create a musical surprise.[52]

Pat Mora poses with her friend, writer Murray Bodo, in front of an Italian castle. In 2003, Mora was lucky enough to live in this castle for a month. She spent most of her time there writing.

6

Stories About Women

MORA'S CHILDREN'S BOOK *The Night the Moon Fell* is based on an old legend of the Maya Indians of Mexico, which said that one night the moon fell into the sea. The tiniest fish rescued the moon and helped it return to the sky. Once back in the sky, the moon and the fish remained overhead, swimming forever in the Milky Way.

Mora retold the story in her book, but in Mora's version she has portrayed the moon as a woman. Indeed, Mora often assigns female characteristics to objects like the moon, the desert, cactuses, and the mountains in her stories. "The natural world—and we humans are part of it—is a major source of inspiration and strength," said Mora. "I feel blessed to see the power of mountains, to hear the wind's music, to be dazzled by the stars. Mountains, deserts, water, the moon are deep, feminine symbols of strength and endurance."[53]

As a feminist, Mora often portrays women as strong people who make their own decisions. In many of Mora's stories and poems, women rise up to conquer tremendous challenges.

One book for young readers in which Mora makes a definite statement about the power of women is *Doña Flor: A Tall Tale About a Giant Woman With a Great Big Heart.* Published in 2005, the book tells the story of a giant, Doña Flor, who looks out for the safety of her village. Doña Flor has special powers: In addition to being a giant, she can speak every human and animal language, even rattlesnake. When the wind blows so hard that it knocks down trees and houses in the village, Doña Flor tames the wind by giving it a big hug. Then the loud roar of a puma, or a mountain lion, worries the villagers, and Doña Flor tries to calm them by digging a new riverbed with her thumb. These efforts fail to make the villagers happy, so Doña Flor resolves to find the mountain lion and find out why it is roaring so loudly. She heads into the mountains, where deer, snakes, and rabbits guide her, and eventually she finds the puma. The animal startles her with a roar, and Doña Flor jumps so high that she bumps into the sun and gives it a black eye. Finally confronting the lion, Doña Flor finds out that the critter is not ferocious, but just a little cat who enjoys the sound he can make with his roar. Mora wrote, "Doña Flor just smiled at that brave cat and said, 'Why, you're just a kitten to me, Pumito,' and she bent down and scratched that puma behind the ears, and she whispered to him in cat talk until that cat began to purr and *purrrrrrrrr*. Pumito began to lick Flor's face with his wet tongue." (*Doña Flor*)

Finally, Doña Flor and the mountain lion become friends and she convinces him to stop scaring the villagers. At the conclusion of the story, Doña Flor plucks a star from the sky to help the villagers find their way home and then, weary from her adventure with the mountain lion, she makes herself a bed with the clouds and goes to sleep.

According to Mora, *Doña Flor* teaches some important lessons about women and how they solve problems. Instead of searching for the mountain lion with the intention of killing the animal, Doña Flor finds the animal and, after learning that it is as harmless, makes friends with it and convinces it to stop scaring the villagers. The story teaches readers to value all wildlife and to solve their problems with a gentle hand. Mora said,

> It makes me very happy that today teachers use picture books in middle schools and high schools, and they use them to help talk about values. I talk about *Doña Flor* with teachers and librarians because when I decided to write what's called an original tall tale, it was because I felt, "Well, we need some images of an immense and powerful bilingual woman." But if you read the book you notice that it is not through force or violence that she is a good neighbor or that she manages to reach her goals, it's because she has a great big heart and she's generous and she's kind to animals and she can speak their languages, so they give her advice.

They tell her where to go to find the mountain lion that's terrorizing her community.[54]

BEAUTY OF THE DESERT

Doña Flor is among the many women and young girls who serve as central characters in Mora's poems as well as her children's books. As a Latina, Mora feels a responsibility to explore those stories. Indeed, even when she uses metaphors in her poetry, the symbols, such as the desert, often stand for women.

In "Desert Woman," one of the poems in the anthology *My One True Name*, Mora wrote,

> . . . no branches wail
> or whisper our sad songs
> safe behind our thorns.
> Don't be deceived.
> When we bloom, we stun. (*My Own True Name*, p. 55)

In the poem, Mora is not only talking about the dangerous thorns of the desert cactus, but the dangerous thorns of women as well. Mora said that the wind, broiling sun, wildlife, and plant life of the desert could symbolize the many moods and abilities of women. "The desert never ceases to amaze me," she said.

> I took the desert for granted and it was not really until I started writing that I realized that in many ways the desert is one of my mythic women. . . . Those of us who love the desert also know that she's beautiful. All kinds of spirits dance on it; the wind dances on it, and the light dances on it. Part of why she's a mythic woman is the desert's strength. She is a survivor of incredible heat and cold, and sometimes drought. Sometimes

STORIES ABOUT WOMEN

Mora has a special interest in writing about women, whether real or mythical. In A Library for Juana: The World of Sor Juana Inés, *Mora tells the story of Sor Juana Inés de la Cruz (depicted in the painting above), a seventeenth-century nun who was also a poet, playwright, and songwriter.*

you have to be attentive to see the desert's beauty. She is incredibly beautiful."[55]

Many of the women that Mora has written about are mythical: for example, Doña Flor and the woman in "Desert Woman." Mora has also chronicled the lives of some real women who have played important roles in the history of Mexico or in Mexican American culture. Mora's 2002 book, *A Library for Juana: The World of Sor Juana Inés*, tells the story of Sor Juana Inés de la Cruz, a seventeenth-century nun who was also a poet, playwright, and songwriter.

Did you know...

Born in 1648, Juana Inés de la Cruz learned to read at the age of three during an era when educational opportunities for girls were rare. Later, a university in Mexico City barred Juana from attending because they didn't allow girls, but she tried to convince her mother to send her disguised as a boy. When her mother refused, Sor Juana resolved to educate herself.

Sor Juana studied Latin, but whenever she believed she was not learning fast enough, she would cut off a lock of hair. She later wrote, "I cut off the hair in punishment for my head's ignorance, for it didn't seem right to me that a head so naked of knowledge should be dressed up

STORIES ABOUT WOMEN

Although Sor Juana grew up during a period of Mexican history when girls were given few opportunities for education, she learned to read at the age of three and later studied Latin. As a poet, Sor Juana called for equal rights for women. One of her main achievements was that she compiled a library of some 4,000 volumes at a time when there were no more than a handful of books in the American colonies to the north. "How sad that I never heard about her when I was in school and college, but when I did finally discover her brilliant essay on women's right to an intellectual life, I became fascinated by a woman

with hair. For knowledge is a more desirable adornment."*

At the age of 21, Juana entered the Convent of the Order of St. Jerome in Mexico City, where she took her vows as a nun. She also wrote poetry and plays, and she established an impressive library of more than 4,000 volumes at the convent. For many years, however, church officials opposed her call for women's education, and she was ordered to stop writing in 1693. Sor Juana died in 1695 as a plague swept through the convent.

* Quoted in "Sor Juana Inés de la Cruz." http://oregonstate.edu/instruct/phl302/philosophers/cruz.html.

determined to learn to read at the ripe old age of three,"[56] said Mora.

Book critics praised *A Library for Juana*. Writing in *Horn Book*, critic Mary M. Burns said,

> Juana's triumphs as a scholar and writer, her decision to become a nun so that she could find the time necessary to pursue her chosen work, and her success in creating one of the largest libraries in the Americas demonstrates that she was indeed a remarkable woman. Moreover, she is portrayed as fun-loving, energetic, and creative.[57]

Mora has also written a poem about Sor Juana, titled "The Young Sor Juana." The poem begins,

> *I'm three and cannot play away my days*
> *to suit my sweet mamá. Sleep well, my dolls,*
> *for I must run to school behind my sister's frowns.*
> *for I must learn to unknit words and letters, to knit them new*
> *with my own hand.*[58]

NOTABLE ARTISTS

Another notable woman who was featured by Mora in a book is Maria Hesch, an artist from Sante Fe, New Mexico, who spent decades painting scenes of the New Mexico countryside. Hesch's work is often compared to that of a much more renowned artist, Anna Mary Robertson, who was known as Grandma Moses. Like Grandma Moses, Hesch painted sweeping and colorful vistas of rural life that depicted ordinary people going about the simple business of living their lives.

Mora's book *Maria Paints the Hills* was published in 2002 and is illustrated with many of Hesch's paintings.

Mora tells the story from the viewpoint of Maria as a young girl as she learns to appreciate the colors and shapes of the landscape. In the book, Mora describes how Maria gazes into a fire and imagines that the flames have taken the shape of tiny toy horses, or *caballitos*, jumping in and out of the fire. In the book, Mora wrote, "'Look, Tía,' Maria says excitedly. 'See the caballitos galloping in the fire? The flames look like little horses.'" (*Maria Paints the Hills*)

Mora discovered Hesch's work after she visited the Museum of International Folk Art in Santa Fe. She was dazzled by the artwork, finding it both comforting and relaxing. "It lowers my blood pressure," she said. ("Immigrants," p. 221) Hesch's work inspired Mora to write a picture book about the artist, and she believed Hesch's paintings should be used to illustrate the story. "I thought the art would make a wonderful children's book . . . about the past and how people lived then," said Mora.[59]

Another renowned Latino woman whom Mora has featured in her work is the Mexican artist Frida Kahlo, whose story is told in Mora's book of poetry titled *Agua Santa/Holy Water*. Kahlo is a tragic figure. Born in 1907, she aspired to a career as a physician but was seriously injured in a bus accident in 1925, which left her unable to have children. After spending months in the hospital, Kahlo decided to give up the study of medicine and instead seek a career as an artist. Kahlo endured a stormy marriage to Mexican artist Diego Rivera, and she painted dark portraits, many of which show her pain and depression. She was sympathetic to the communist movement and is reputed to have had a love affair with Leon Trotsky, the exiled Russian communist leader who was murdered in 1940 on the orders of Soviet Union dictator Joseph

Stalin. In the poem titled "Dear Frida," Mora wrote about a troubled and tortured woman. She wrote, "Your paintings don't laugh like you do. . . .Your wounds are always open, Frida. . . .You are your art, and you make us watch you die." (*Agua Santa/Holy Water*, pp. 51–52)

TWO INDEPENDENT WOMEN

Many of the girls and women featured in Mora's stories and poems are based on her own family members, including her mother, who is portrayed by the character Estelita, in *The Rainbow Tulip*, and her aunt Lobo, the elderly aunt in *A Birthday Basket for Tía*. According to Mora, her beliefs in the power of women stem from her admiration for her mother and her Aunt Lobo. Estela Delgado sought education, learned to speak English and Spanish, and excelled in public speaking. "My mother was a powerful woman because she believed in herself and she always had the vocabulary to state her beliefs,"[60] said Mora.

Her aunt Lobo was also a strong and independent woman. She never married and, indeed, did not need a husband to guide her through life. As she grew up under the guidance of these two very independent women, Mora said, she became convinced that women can be independent and strong. She explained,

> I began my life with the image that women are equals to men, that they can think well, that books are a part of their lives and help them be independent and help them to be able to state their beliefs well. And that has affected how I feel about everything from who can be the president of a university or who could be the president of the United States. It is a surprise to me that people still think it would be in some way odd for a woman to be president of the United States. It surprises me

because I begin with the assumption that men and women both can think and it has nothing to do with whether their gender is male or female.[61]

Pat Mora's daughters, Cissy (left) and Libby pose with her son Bill (left) and her son-in-law Roger in 1996. Family is very important to Mora, who told the stories of her own family in the book House of Houses.

7

Stories About Families

PART OF THE tradition of being a Latina is to hold family life in high esteem, which is why so many of Mora's stories and poems feature strong family environments. Certainly, the female figure in the home has long been a central figure in Mora's work, but she also writes about the relationships between fathers and sons, uncles and nephews, and grandfathers and grandsons.

Mora's children's book *Pablo's Tree* tells the story of an adopted boy named Pablo, who spends his birthday with his grandfather Lito. Each year, when Pablo comes to visit, Lito decorates a tree for Pablo, which he planted on the day Pablo's mother adopted him. Pablo is surprised by the decorations his grandfather has placed on the tree. In the book, Pablo says, "When I see my tree, I run to it. I touch the tiny colored bells and wind chimes. 'Ooooh,' I say. I run around the tree, touching the bells and chimes. The wind blows and my tree jingles and rings." (*Pablo's Tree*)

Pablo's Tree illustrates how Pablo's mother and grandfather show their love to the boy. Lito has cared for the tree by picking just the right place to plant the sapling and giving it plenty of water and sunshine, and the tree has grown tall and strong in the five years since Pablo was adopted. Clearly, the tree is a metaphor for Pablo: With care and love, a boy, just like a tree, can grow tall and strong. In the story, Pablo says, "And the tree grew and grew. Like me." (*Pablo's Tree*)

GROWTH OF THE FAMILY

From her earliest days as a poet, Mora has concentrated on family experiences, often using metaphors to describe the experiences of growing up and the influences of family members on her life. In her poem "The Desert Is My Mother," which also became a picture book, Mora wrote that the desert can provide the same type of nurturing and comfort that a mother can provide. For example, the desert can feed her with a "red prickly pear on a spiked cactus" and can comfort her by taking her in her arms. When Mora wants the desert to sing to her, the desert responds with "windy songs," and when Mora wants the desert to make her beautiful,

> She offers turquoise for my fingers,
> a pink blossom for my hair. (*My Own True Name*, p. 18)

STORIES ABOUT FAMILIES

Sometimes, when Mora talks about family members, metaphors are unnecessary. Her poem "Teenagers" describes a mother's memories of watching her children grow into young adults. She wrote, "I see faces I once held. . . . I see familiar skin now stretched on long bodies." (*My Own True Name*, p. 24) In "Family Ties," Mora described how a friend's grandmother sewed white uniforms for cannery workers and often gave her granddaughter similar uniforms as gifts, even though the girl preferred to wear designer blue jeans and other expensive clothes:

> *But when I shyly showed my abuelita*
> *my good report card or recited the Pledge of Allegiance,*
> *my grandmother would smile and hand me a uniform,*
> *never the right size, but a gift*
> *I would add to the white stack*
> *at the bottom of my closet.* (*My Own True Name*, p. 22)

Mora's books for children also focused on family life. In addition to *Pablo's Tree*, some of her other family-oriented books for young readers include *A Birthday Basket for Tía, The Bakery Lady,* and *The Rainbow Tulip.* After several years of writing poetry and children's books about families, Mora started to think about her own family. She realized that there were stories to tell about the Moras and the Delgados and their experiences in the United States. In 1997, her thoughts coalesced into the book *House of Houses*, which is a memoir of Mora's family and her years growing up in El Paso. Mora described why the book was important to her:

> I became keenly interested in family stories when I was working on our family memoirs, *House of Houses*. Although I had

written individual poems about an aunt or uncle previously, working on our family story increased my curiosity about the stories of other families. . . . Being Mexican American, I come from a culture in which family is very important, and the metaphor of family is very important to me, our family in this country, our family on the planet.[62]

EXTENSIVE MEMOIR

House of Houses is, of course, all about the growth of one family. It is an extensive memoir of the lives of Mora's

Did you know...

Parents of young students often participate in their children's education. They attend parent–teacher conferences, assist on class trips, and enjoy parent–student activities that many schools schedule in the evenings. Pat Mora has found, though, that sometimes Latino parents are hesitant to get involved with their children's schools.

According to Mora, Latino parents traditionally have a great respect for schools and believe teachers know what is best for their children. Many Latinos may also be hesitant to talk to teachers or attend conferences about their children, however, because they may not speak English.

Mora has worked hard to convince Latino parents to be partners in their children's education. She has also worked to show the schools that they have a responsibility to immediate family members and ancestors. The first page of the book includes her family tree, where Mora has traced her ancestors back to some of her great great-grandparents, who lived in Mexico in the nineteenth century. Inside, readers will find a photograph of a great-uncle who rode with revolutionaries during the Mexican Revolution of 1910. There are also many photographs of other members of Mora's family who have become famous through her books and poetry, including her parents, Raúl and Estela Mora, and her Aunt Lobo, Ignacia Delgado. In the photo, Aunt

> involve Latino parents: to emphasize bilingual activities in school or to encourage Latino parents to talk to classes about their culture.
>
> "We're cheating ourselves if we don't realize that these parents can be our teachers and our students' teachers, and bring them into the classroom and involve them. And my experience is that they just glow when that happens," said Mora. "So, the myth that somehow Latino parents can't be invited in and can't be active and excited members of the school community is a dangerous myth. And I think we need to put it to rest—and be busy building those bridges."*
>
> * Quoted in "Transcript From an Interview With Pat Mora," Reading Rockets. http://www.readingrockets.org/books/interviews/mora/transcript.

Lobo is a smartly dressed and elegant middle-aged woman holding a bouquet of flowers, who looks very different from the elderly aunt that Mora chose to write about in *A Birthday Basket for Tía*. In *House of Houses*, Mora said she tries to show the many sides of her family and how they influenced her work as a writer.

"It's not a book that I ever intended to write," Mora said of *House of Houses*, "but I come from a very close family, and a lot of my children's books have family themes. So *House of Houses* was a way to spend time thinking about some of the most important voices in my life, which is why I think family stories are so important."[63]

House of Houses is separated into 12 chapters, and Mora has named each chapter for a different month. Some of the stories Mora tells in the book are quite humorous. For example, she recounts how her father loved the sport of boxing so much that, as a young boy in El Paso, he found a way to sneak into boxing matches by telling the ticket takers that he worked as a newspaper reporter. At the time, Raúl Mora was nothing more than a newsboy who sold newspapers. When he got to the arena, he noticed that some men were admitted for free if they said the word "press" to the ticket takers, so 10-year-old Raúl tried it. He simply walked up to the ticket window, held up a bundle of newspapers, said "press," and was admitted for free. In the book, Mora wrote that her father "chuckles now at himself, sitting on those papers to watch his gloved heroes, wondering what the ticket takers thought of the boy he was." (*House of Houses,* p. 85)

Another humorous story involves Mora's maternal grandfather, Eduardo Luis Delgado. Mora's Uncle Lalo relates the story to her. As a young man, Lalo said, Mora's

STORIES ABOUT FAMILIES

Pat Mora (second from left) poses with her siblings: (left to right) Stella, Anthony, and Cissy. The traditions of her family helped them to remain close-knit over the years, and Mora's stories about families often reflect this.

grandfather and his friends were walking home after a night at a tavern when they came upon a cemetery. All of the men were frightened to enter the cemetery, except one. On a dare, the courageous man agreed to enter, walk to the far end of the cemetery, and stab a cane into the ground. Eduardo and the other men planned to return in the daytime; if they saw the cane standing in the ground, they would know that their friend had been brave enough to walk to the far end.

The courageous fellow entered the cemetery while his friends waited at the entrance. After several minutes, their friend did not return. The other men grew concerned, and they finally found the courage to go in after him. They stumbled through the cemetery in the dark and came across their friend, "sprawled out cold on the ground." In the book, Mora continued:

> "Now what happened," my uncle chuckles, "is that the first man had on a long cape, and when he stabs that cane into the ground, he plunges the cane into his cape. When he turns to leave, he can't, feels something—someone—pullin' at him from the grave, and he's so scared, he faints." (*House of Houses*, p. 260)

TOUCHING MOMENTS

There are also some touching moments in the book. Mora tells about Raúl Mora's grandmother, her great-grandmother Tomasa, who died in her 90s. Raúl was very fond of his *abuela,* the Spanish word for grandmother, and he was heartbroken when she grew ill. At the age of 12, Raúl came home one night after delivering his newspapers to find his grandmother frail and near death. When the others left her room, Raúl tried to lift his grandmother out of bed, but as he lifted the frail old woman, he believed she had died in his arms. He placed her back down, and then sat by her bed until his mother ordered him to leave her room. In the book, Mora wrote,

> "The next morning," my father says, "I go to check on her, and Tomasa's bed is empty. I get so scared. I think: she died, *mi abuelita* who loved me so much is gone, and they've taken her body. I feel awful.
>
> "Then I hear pans in the kitchen. I walk in there, and there's *mi abuela* cooking eggs and (sausage). She lives another five years." (*House of Houses*, p. 260)

Book critics delivered high praise for *House of Houses*. Writing in the *Library Journal,* critic Susan Dearstyne said,

STORIES ABOUT FAMILIES

Pat Mora poses with her husband, Dr. Vernon Scarborough, a professor of archaeology with a specialty in the Maya Indians. The couple married in 1984.

"These 12 chapters, one for each month of the year, are deeply meaningful; each story, event, and name has a message about life, love, dependence, and memory."[64] A critic for *Publishers Weekly* said, "Mora's poetic biography reads like fiction—it is a cacophony of sound, a prism of light, a lattice of memories that is sometimes magical. It is a family portrait spilling over the framework of a house, '*la casa de casas.*'...This is a book the reader will need to sink into but the reward is a head full of indelible images."[65]

To write *House of Houses*, Mora returned to El Paso to interview many of her relatives and traveled to Los Angeles to interview her mother and her sister Stella. When she interviewed her mother, she learned about Estela's experience as a young girl participating in the May Day parade, when she wore the tulip costume of many colors. That story led to Mora's writing *The Rainbow Tulip*. "When I finished *House of Houses*, I thought, 'Well, I'm going to take that story out and do it as a picture book,'" she recalled.[66]

In fact, Mora learned so much about her family that she could not fit all of the stories into *House of Houses*. She kept many notes from her interviews, though, and hopes to use the stories in books for young readers in years to come.

Although *House of Houses* is told in a series of chapters written in prose, Mora does use many metaphors to describe the lives of her family members and the institution of the family itself. In the book, the Mora family is a "house." The house is made of sturdy adobe walls that keep it upright, just as families have sturdy fathers, mothers, sons, and daughters. Guests may come and go, just as family members and friends come and go. A courtyard garden is in the center of the house, which is the life that gives the family its strength. In the book, Mora clearly uses the old stone home at 704 Mesita Street in El Paso to describe her family:

> So much intellectual weight for this home rising through and from generations. I strike a rounded adobe mantle above a snapping fire, feel protective of this house that grows naturally in the Chihuahua desert, protects and mothers me, lets me listen, shed the layers I wear outside. . . .
>
> Why in my fifties did I decide to explore this house and its garden? I needed a place to put the stories and the voices

before they vanished like blooms and leaves will vanish on the wind outside, voices which, perceived as ordinary, would be unprotected, blown into oblivion. Since the family isn't together geographically, using the tools I know, I created a place welcoming to our spirits. . . . (*House of Houses*, p. 272)

As a little girl, Pat Mora loved to read—she is shown here (left) reading with a classmate in elementary school. As an adult, Mora has made many efforts to encourage other children to read, including establishing a national day to recognize the importance of reading called El Día de los Niños/El Día de los Libros *("Children's Day/Book Day").*

8

Promoting Literacy in America

MORA'S 1997 BOOK *Tomás and the Library Lady* tells the story of a young Mexican-American boy who is the son of migrant farm workers. In the winter, his parents pick fruit and vegetables on Texas farms, and in the summer they work on farms in Iowa. Tomás and his family do not have a real home, only the barracks they share with other farm workers and the car they use to travel from farm to farm. "Year after year," Mora wrote, "they bump-bumped along in their rusty old car." (*Tomás and the Library Lady*)

Tomás has a burning desire to learn, and he pesters his grandfather to tell him stories. One summer, while the family is working in Iowa, his Papá Grande runs out of new stories to tell Tomás. He tells his grandson to go to the library in town and read books so he can learn his own stories. Wrote Mora,

> The next morning Tomás walked downtown. He looked at the big library. Its tall windows were like eyes glaring at him. Tomás walked around and around the big building. He saw children coming out carrying books. Slowly he started climbing up, up the steps. He counted them to himself in Spanish. *Uno, dos, tres, cuatro. . . .* His mouth felt full of cotton. (*Tomás and the Library Lady*)

The librarian sees Tomás peering in through the window, and she invites him to come inside, where she asks him what he likes to read. Tomás responds that he is interested in learning about tigers and dinosaurs, so the librarian finds Tomás some books that interest him, and thus introduces the boy to the world of books. Each day that summer, Tomás returns to the library, where he sits quietly and reads books. The librarian also lets him take books back to the farm workers' barracks, where he reads the stories to his family. In return, Tomás teaches the librarian a few words of Spanish. "Tomás would smile," Mora wrote in the book. "He liked being the teacher. The library lady pointed to a book. 'Book is *libro*,' said Tomás." (*Tomás and the Library Lady*)

Finally the summer ends, and Tomás and his family must return to Texas. As a parting gift, Tomás gives the librarian a loaf of bread his mother has baked. The librarian gives Tomás a gift as well: a book, which Tomás reads in the car,

PROMOTING LITERACY IN AMERICA

all the way back to Texas. "That night, bumping along again in the tired old car, Tomás held a shiny new book, a present from the library lady," Mora wrote. "Papá Grande smiled and said, 'More stories for the new storyteller.'" (*Tomás and the Library Lady*)

Mora believes *Tomás and the Library Lady* is one of the most important books she has written for young Latino readers and about the importance of educators. The story illustrates the importance of reading to all children, and shows that all children can find great pleasure in books. She said,

> The book is about this journey that [Tomás] makes. Throughout the book, he's a child but he has had a transforming experience. And, of course, I believe in the power of teachers and librarians with my whole heart. And in many ways, this book embodies that—that because of this *one* person who is there for him, who takes an interest in him, who helps him with his reading—and in the book I have him teach her Spanish, because I want that notion of balance, that we're both learning.[67]

What makes *Tomás and the Library Lady* particularly poignant is that it is based on a true story. The character of Tomás is actually Texas-born Tomás Rivera, the son of migrant farm workers. He rose to become the chancellor, or head, of the University of California at Riverside. Before he died in 1984, Rivera related the story of how a kindly librarian in a small Iowa town introduced him to the world of books. Today, the university's library bears his name.

Certainly, as the son of migrant farm workers, Rivera had to struggle to succeed. Indeed, after graduating from college with a degree in English, his first job was driving a school bus. "His secret, though, was that he kept learning," Mora said. "And that's what I tell students. He kept learning. He kept getting more and more degrees. And, eventually, he was a faculty member, and then he was a vice president. And then he became the president of the University of California at Riverside."[68]

"BOOKJOY"

Tomás and the Library Lady illustrates the importance that Mora places on literacy. She has devoted several years to promoting literacy among young people, particularly young Latinos. In fact, this was a driving force behind her decision to start to write children's books. *Tomás and the Library Lady* was the first picture book that Mora wrote that was accepted for publication. Its publication was delayed because the publisher rejected many of the illustrations that were submitted by artists for the story. Finally, *Tomás and the Library Lady* was published in 1997 after the publisher selected artist Raul Colón to illustrate the story. Colón and Mora also collaborated on *Doña Flor: A Tall Tale About a Giant Woman With a Great Big Heart*.

In addition to writing books, Mora has done even more to promote literacy. In 1996, she founded *El Día de los Niños/ El Día de los Libros* as a national day of recognition for the importance of children and reading. In English, the words mean "Childrens' Day/Book Day." The day is celebrated on April 30 each year and includes events throughout the country. In explaining her motivation behind establishing the national day, Mora said:

> We all have responsibility. We have the responsibility to vote, and we also have the responsibility to help shape our city or

our neighborhood or state. However we want it to work, we have responsibilities to make this a better world, not sit around and gripe about it.

But we have to think about, what is it that we feel strongly about? What do we want to be an advocate for? Some people feel very strongly that we should be protecting the forests, and so they are advocates for the natural world. I did not start out my adult life thinking that I was going to end up being an advocate for literacy. I was a teacher, and I was a university administrator and museum director before I became a writer.

But it was really only after I had spent time writing and spent time visiting schools and spent time thinking about the fact that I am very lucky. I grew up in a home with books, I grew up in a home where my parents supported reading and were fans of the public library. So I am very fortunate that I have experienced and always had what I call bookjoy: That private pleasure of sitting down with a good book. It makes me sad that there are children across the world, in this country too, who may not have a single book in their home. So I got very intrigued by how teachers and librarians and parents could celebrate children and could celebrate linking children and books.[69]

Mora said she conceived the idea for El Día de los Niños/El Día de los Libros when she learned that in Mexico there is a holiday known as *El Día del Niño*, which means "The Day of the Child." The holiday, which is celebrated each year on April 30, includes activities at home and in schools where parents and teachers plan special treats for young children. After learning about El Día del Niño, Mora talked to some educators, librarians, and friends about establishing a similar day in the United States, but altering it to

Mora is shown here speaking in Arizona when her book Confetti *was selected as the Governor's Book in 2004. The Governor's Book is part of a program in which the governor of Arizona selects one children's book to be distributed for free to children across the state, in order to emphasize the importance of reading for even the youngest children.*

emphasize literacy. Soon, Mora had developed the celebration as El Día de los Niños/El Día de los Libros to spread what she calls "bookjoy."

Mora said that El Día de los Niños/El Día de los Libros is known mostly in its shortened title, which is simply *Día*, which means "day." Said Mora, "It's daily work—and we say every day is *Día* and every day we want to be linking all children with books, languages, and cultures, and then we celebrate together across the country, on April 30."[70]

AWARD WINNERS

Each year, libraries, schools, and other organizations that provide educational opportunities for young people are encouraged to conduct programs specifically aimed at promoting family reading. To encourage participation, Mora, her brother Anthony, and sisters Cecilia and Stella have established the "Estela and Raúl Mora Award." Named in honor of their parents, the award is presented to the organization that provides an example of exemplary participation in Día.

The 2006 winner of the award, which includes a plaque and cash prize, was the Salt Lake City, Utah, chapter of the National Association to Promote Library and Information Services to Latinos. ("REFORMA"). In Salt Lake City, where the Latino population has grown by more than 20 percent during the past few years, REFORMA, assisted by the Salt Lake City Public Library, staged 10 bilingual children's events at the Utah Cultural Celebration Center. Attendance at the event numbered more than 4,000 participants, who had the opportunity to compete in a Spanish spelling bee, as well as contests for young writers, poets, and illustrators. Latino artists provided demonstrations, and each child who attended the program left with a free book.

Día is, of course, for more than just Latino children. Children from all cultures are encouraged to participate so that they can learn about Latino and other cultures as well as the importance of literacy in Spanish, English, and other home languages. For example, in Kenton County, Kentucky, the community participated in a project to record the stories of local immigrants in a single volume.

According to Mora, participation in Día has grown tremendously since she founded the event more than a decade ago. Groups that have competed recently for the award are located across the country, including Florida, Massachusetts, and California. She said,

> The important thing is that it's work that we do every day of the year, and it is growing and growing and growing. I was talking to someone in Michigan, and they said, 'Oh, we've been celebrating *Día* for three years at the public library!' Of course, every time I hear that, I'm happy. I do work at it all the time, as do other people. I mean to be an

Did you know...

Tomás and the Library Lady sends a message to young readers about the importance of reading, but the book also tells another story: that of the migrant farm workers.

In the book, Tomás and his family travel from farm to farm looking for work. Tomás's parents have to work long hours for low wages.

American literature has chronicled the plight of farm workers many times in American literature, beginning with John Steinbeck's landmark 1939 novel, *The Grapes of Wrath*. More important, the Latino labor leader Cesar Chavez struggled for decades to win higher wages for migrant farm workers.

Still, Mora believes that many young people do not understand how fruits and vegetables find their way into grocery stores and are unfamiliar with the term "migrant farm workers." She explained, advocate, you don't just come up with a good idea and let it go.[71]

Día is now housed at the Association for Library Service to Children (ALSC), a division of the American Library Association (ALA).

FUTURE PROJECTS

To promote Día, as well as her other efforts to improve literacy in America, Mora maintains a busy travel schedule

> Most students today do not know what those words mean. School after school, I say, "What are migrant workers?" And unless the teacher has done work before my visit, students do not know that. They are growing up believing that those strawberries and tomatoes arrive at the store on their own. So, it's important that people realize that there is really hard stoop labor, and that the living conditions of migrant workers are still deplorable. And we're talking about right in our own country. And the way migrant students can be treated in schools can still be sort of an embarrassment.*
>
> * Quoted in "Transcript From an Interview With Pat Mora," Reading Rockets. http://www.readingrockets.org/books/interviews/mora/transcript.

that takes her across the country. Indeed, each year she makes dozens of public appearances, speaking at conferences and visiting colleges and schools.

There is no question, though, that Mora is still busy writing. She juggles many projects at a time, and publishers have scheduled releases of her work years in advance. In late 2006, Mora released a sixth collection of poems titled *Adobe Odes*. Although the book of 49 poems pays tribute to many ordinary things Mora likes, such as chocolate, books, and dandelions, there are also poems that explore some familiar Mora themes, including families and life along the border.

Mora also wrote *¡Marimba! Animales A–Z*, a picture book that teaches young readers the alphabet and cognates—words that are the same in English and Spanish, such as gorilla and *gorila*.

Another book of poems for children Mora has written is titled *Yum! ¡Mmm! ¡Qué Rico!* The book's poems celebrate 12 native foods of the Americas. The poems have been written in the style of verse known as haiku, which are short poems told in three lines. She said,

> I had never played with haiku very much. One of the things I try to do as a writer is always look for a good idea, and I try to take notes of good ideas and I know teachers love to teach haikus. You can do haiku whether you're working with second-graders or graduate students. I also love indigenous plants, indigenous foods and indigenous people. So I decided I would try to do a book of haiku about the plants and the foods of the Americas. It was fun to think about what type of haiku kids would like to read. I thought about blueberries and ice cream.[72]

Another upcoming book is *Abuelos*. Mora has often written about *abuelos*, or grandfathers, in her poetry and storybooks. Recently, though, she discovered another, tradition for the word, as Mora explained:

> When I first got to New Mexico, I began hearing another meaning for the word *abuelo*—that a long time ago, in small, northern New Mexico communities, on cold December nights there was this belief that furry and sooty mountain men would come down to check on the children to make sure they were minding their parents and not going in the river at night, or not saying their prayers. Once it got near December, children would be wondering, "When are the *abuelos* going to come?" Communities would build bonfires, and usually there was a party afterwards. It had almost a Halloween sense of scary but fun. And I thought, "Oh, that might make a great picture book."[73]

Mora's book about this custom is slated for publication in 2008.

Starting in 2008, Mora plans to introduce a four-book series titled *My Family/Mi Familia*. The books will be written in Spanish and English, and tell the stories of the Rosas family and their children, Isabel, Tina, and Danny. According to Mora, the books are planned for very young readers because,

> I realized that if I went into a bookstore, not only did I see very few, if any, books about Latino families, I wasn't seeing any bilingual books that were easy reads—that the family could read together, the way we would read *Goodnight Moon*, with very simple text. So I thought, "That would be fun because families could read it in English, they could

read it in Spanish, they could read it in both. And I thought it might be fun to do it as a series. The series is about one family because I thought sometimes kids like to get used to certain characters."[74]

Mora expects two of the *My Family/Mi Familia* books to be released in 2008, and the other two are scheduled for release in 2009. Another new release is *Join Hands!*, a book of poetry about diverse Americans and their families that will be illustrated with photographs. Mora has also written a Christmas book, titled *A Piñata in a Pine Tree*, which will be a Latino version of the classic Christmas poem "The Twelve Days of Christmas." This song, originating in England, celebrates the gift giving that begins on Christmas Day, December 25, and ends 12 days later on January 5, the night before the Epiphany, which is also known as the Feast of the Three Kings.

According to Mora, the Epiphany, which falls on January 6, is a very important holiday in Latin America. Although the classic poem mentions such gifts as a "three French hens, two turtle doves, and a partridge in a pear tree," Mora's book will describe some gifts that Latinos are more likely to give during Christmastime, such as bells, birds, and tamales (doughy cornmeal snacks).

STORIES STAY WITH HER READERS

Mora has written a book to celebrate reading and promote El Día de los Niños/El Día de los Libros. Scheduled for release in 2009, *Book Fiesta! El Día de los Niños/El Día de los Libros* (tentative title) will illustrate how books can be enjoyed anywhere, even in a hot air balloon. In the book, Mora will include an author's note that explains the history of Día and will also suggest activities that educators, librarians, and others can stage to promote reading by young people.

Over the years, Mora has told stories of the desert, influential Latinos from history, strong-willed women, and families that manage to stay together through some very trying ordeals. Mora hopes the books and poems she writes for her readers stay with them long after they finish the stories:

> Will [my books] find a place in people's hearts, for it's that soft yet sturdy home I want for my books. Although I write and speak about the importance of having books by Latinos in libraries, bookstores, and schools, and I do think that it is vital in our multicultural society, secretly I want my books not only in public spaces, but also in private places. I want the books to live long lives deep inside the reader.[75]

CHRONOLOGY

1942 Patricia Estella Mora is born on January 19 in El Paso, Texas.

1956 Mora receives a typewriter from her parents in the eighth grade as a graduation gift; she begins to write poetry.

1960 Mora graduated from high school; she enrolls in Texas Western College.

1963 Mora graduates from college; she marries and takes a job as a public school teacher.

1966 Mora sells a story idea for $100 to the Hallmark greeting card company; the book is never published.

1971 Mora joins the faculty of El Paso Community College.

1981 Mora transfers to college administration to devote more time to writing; she publishes her first poem in a Latino anthology; Mora and her husband agree to divorce.

1984 *Chants*, Mora's first book of poetry is published; she marries Vernon Scarborough.

1989 Mora resigns from the university and moves to Cincinnati with second husband to be a consultant and full-time writer.

1992 *A Birthday Basket for Tía*, Mora's first children's book is published.

1993 Raúl Mora, her father, dies.

1994 *Pablo's Tree* is published.

1995 *Agua Santa: Holy Water* is published.

1996 Mora establishes El Día de los Niños/El Día de los Libros as an annual celebration to promote literacy.

1997 *House of Houses*, Mora's memoir of her family and childhood in El Paso, and *Tomás and the Library Lady* are published.

1998 *This Big Sky* is published.

1999 *The Rainbow Tulip* is published.

2001 *My Own True Name: New and Selected Poems for Young Adults*, Mora's first book of poetry for teenage readers is published.

CHRONOLOGY

2002 *A Library for Juana: The World of Sor Juana Inés* and *Maria Paints the Hills* are published.

2005 *Doña Flor: A Tall Tale About a Giant Woman With a Great Big Heart* and *The Song of Francis and the Animals* are published.

2006 Mora publishes *Adobe Odes and ¡Marimba! Animales A–Z*.

2007 *Yum!¡Mmm!¡Qué Rico!* is published.

NOTES

Chapter 1

1. "*A Birthday Basket for Tiá*," *Publishers Weekly* (Aug. 31, 1992).
2. Quoted in Scot Peacock, ed., *Something About the Author,* vol. 134. Farmington Hills, Mich.: Gale Group, 2003, p. 116.
3. Quoted in Connie C. Rockman, ed., *Eighth Book of Junior Authors and Illustrators*. New York: H.W. Wilson, 2000, p. 377.

Chapter 2

4. Quoted in Marty Racine, "Award-Winning Writer Glides Between Two Worlds," *Houston Chronicle* (May 30, 1999): p. 1-F.
5. Ibid.
6. Ibid.
7. Quoted in Scot Peacock, ed., *Contemporary Authors New Revision Series*, vol. 112 Farmington Hills, Mich.: Thomson Gale, 2003, p. 235.
8. Quoted in Rockman, ed., *Eighth Book of Junior Authors and Illustrators*, p. 377.
9. Quoted in Peacock, ed., *Contemporary Authors New Revision Series*, vol. 112, p. 235.
10. Ibid.
11. Quoted in Rockman, ed., *Eighth Book of Junior Authors and Illustrators*, p. 377.
12. Quoted in "Pat Mora's Interview Transcript." Scholastic. www.teacher.scholastic.com/activities/hispanic/moratscript.htm.
13. Quoted in Racine, "Award-Winning Writer Glides Between Two Worlds," p. 1-F.
14. Quoted in Peacock, ed., *Something About the Author,* vol. 134, p. 115.
15. Ibid.
16. Quoted in Peacock, ed., *Contemporary Authors New Revision Series*, vol. 112, p. 235.
17. Quoted from *Revista Chicano-Riqueña*, in www.patmora.com/book_pages/chants.htm.

Chapter 3

18. Quoted in Darwin L. Henderson, "Listening to the Desert: A Conversation With Pat Mora," *Ohio Journal of the English Language Arts* 41, no. 1 (Fall 2000): p. 12.
19. Quoted in "Transcript from an Interview with Pat Mora," Reading Rockets. www.readingrockets.org/books/interviews/mora/transcript.
20. Ibid.
21. Quoted in Scot Peacock, ed., *Contemporary Authors New Revision Series,* vol. 81. Farmington Hills, Mich.: Gale Group, 1999, p. 272.

NOTES

22. Quoted in Elisabeth Mermann-Jozwiak and Nancy Sullivan, "Interview with Pat Mora," *MELUS* 28, no. 2 (Summer 2003): p. 139.
23. Interview with Pat Mora by Hal Marcovitz, October 25, 2006.
24. Ibid.
25. Ibid.
26. Ibid.

Chapter 4

27. Quoted in Henderson, "Listening to the Desert: A Conversation With Pat Mora," p. 13.
28. Pat Mora, "20 Tips for Writing Children's Books." http://www.patmora.com.
29. Quoted in *Pat Mora: Meet the Mentor*, VHS, Scholastic, 1996.
30. Quoted in Henderson, "Listening to the Desert: A Conversation With Pat Mora," p. 14.
31. Quoted in "Creativity Survey III," Lee & Low Booktalk. www.leeandlow.com/booktalk/create1b.html.
32. Quoted in *Pat Mora: Meet the Mentor*, VHS, Scholastic, 1996.
33. Ibid.
34. Ibid.
35. Ibid.
36. Quoted in Versace Candelora, "Pat Mora: Bringing the Latino Experience to Children's Literature," *Santa Fe New Mexican* (Oct. 6, 1996): p. D-5.
37. Quoted in "Transcript from an Interview with Pat Mora," www.readingrockets.org/books/interviews/mora/transcript.
38. Ibid.
39. Mora, "20 Tips for Writing Children's Books."
40. Quoted in "Creativity Survey III," www.leeandlow.com/booktalk/create1b.html.

Chapter 5

41. Interview With Pat Mora by Hal Marcovitz, October 25, 2006.
42. Ibid.
43. Quoted in Peacock, ed., *Contemporary Authors New Revision Series*, vol. 81, p. 271.
44. Interview with Pat Mora by Hal Marcovitz, October 25, 2006.
45. Ibid.
46. Quoted in Mermann-Jozwiak and Sullivan, "Interview with Pat Mora," p. 139.
47. Quoted in William Balassi, John F. Crawford, and Annie O. Esturoy, eds., *This Is About Vision: Interviews With Southwestern Writers*. Albuquerque: University of New Mexico Press, 1990, pp. 135–136.
48. Quoted in Mermann-Jozwiak and Sullivan, "Interview with Pat Mora," p. 139.
49. Interview with Pat Mora by Hal Marcovitz, October 25, 2006.
50. Ibid.
51. Ibid.
52. Quoted in Lee Bennett Hopkins, "Pat Mora," *Teaching K-8* 36, no. 4 (January 2006): p. 61.

NOTES

Chapter 6

53 Quoted in Aline Pereira. "Interview with Pat Mora," Paper Tigers. www.papertigers.org/interviews/archived_interviews/pmora.html.

54 Interview with Pat Mora by Hal Marcovitz, October 25, 2006.

55 Quoted in Henderson, "Listening to the Desert: A Conversation With Pat Mora," pp. 12–13.

56 Quoted in Susan Lehr, ed., *Beauty, Brains, and Brawn: The Construction of Gender in Children's Literature*. Portsmouth, N.H.: Heinemann, 2001, p. 159.

57 Mary M. Burns, "A Library for Juana: The World of Sor Juana Inés," *Horn Book Magazine* 78, no. 6 (Nov. 1, 2002): p. 778.

58 Quoted in Lehr, ed., *Beauty, Brains, and Brawn: The Construction of Gender in Children's Literature*, p. 159.

59 Ibid.

60 Interview with Pat Mora by Hal Marcovitz, October 25, 2006.

61 Ibid.

Chapter 7

62 Quoted in "An Interview With Pat Mora," *Journal of Adolescent and Adult Literary* 46, no. 2 (October 2002): p. 183.

63 Quoted in "Transcript From an Interview with Pat Mora," www.readingrockets.org/books/interviews/mora/transcript.

64 Susan Dearstyne, "House of Houses," *Library Journal* 122, no. 7 (April 15, 1997): p. 88.

65 Genevieve Stuttaford, Maria Simson, and Jeff Zaleski, "House of Houses," *Publishers Weekly* 244, no. 12 (March 24, 1997): p. 68.

66 Quoted in "Transcript From an Interview with Pat Mora," www.readingrockets.org/books/interviews/mora/transcript.

Chapter 8

67 Quoted in "Transcript From an Interview with Pat Mora," www.readingrockets.org/books/interviews/mora/transcript.

68 Ibid.

69 Interview with Pat Mora by Hal Marcovitz, October 25, 2006.

70 Ibid.

71 Ibid.

72 Ibid.

73 Ibid.

74 Ibid.

75 Quoted in Lehr, ed., *Beauty, Brains, and Brawn: The Construction of Gender in Children's Literature*, p. 158.

WORKS BY PAT MORA

Storybooks

1992 *A Birthday Basket for Tía*
1994 *Listen to the Desert/Oye al Desierto*
1994 *Agua, Agua, Agua*
1994 *Pablo's Tree*
1995 *The Gift of the Poinsettia*
1995 *The Race of Toad and Deer*
1997 *Tomás and the Library Lady*
1998 *Delicious Hullabaloo/Pachanga Deliciosa*
1999 *The Rainbow Tulip*
2000 *The Night the Moon Fell*
2001 *The Bakery Lady/La Señora de la Panadería*
2002 *A Library for Juana: The World of Sor Juana Inés*
2002 *Maria Paints the Hills*
2005 *Doña Flor: A Tall Tale About a Giant Woman With a Great Big Heart*; *The Song of Francis and the Animals*

Books of Poetry

1984 *Chants*
1986 *Borders*
1991 *Communion*
1994 *The Desert Is My Mother/El desierto es mi madre*
1995 *Confetti: Poems for Children*
1995 *Agua Santa: Holy Water*
1996 *Uno, Dos, Tres/One, Two, Three*
1997 *Aunt Carmen's Book of Practical Saints*
1998 *This Big Sky*
2001 *My Own True Name: New and Selected Poems for Young Adults*
2001 *Love to Mamá: A Tribute to Mothers*

2006 *Adobe Odes; ¡Marimba! Animales A-Z*
2007 *Yum! ¡Mmm! ¡Qué Rico!*

Books of Nonfiction
1993 *Nepantla: Essays from the Land in the Middle*
1997 *House of Houses*

Scheduled Releases
2008 *Abuelos; My Family/Mi Familia; Join Hands!*
2009 *Book Fiesta! El Día de los Niños/El Día de los Libros, Children's Day/Book Day*
2009 *A Piñata in a Pine Tree*

POPULAR BOOKS

AGUA SANTA: HOLY WATER
This book of poetry includes Mora's tribute to artist Frida Kahlo, as well as many other poems with feminist themes. Mora also explores Latino culture and family relationships.

THIS BIG SKY
This book of 14 illustrated poems for young readers includes Mora's poem "Old Snake," which helps teach readers that problems are like pesky flies that buzz around the face of the old snake.

A BIRTHDAY BASKET FOR TÍA
Based on a true story in Mora's family, the book tells about a little girl who fills a birthday basket for her *tía*, or aunt, with all the reminders of the good times they share. Mora based the character of Tía on her Aunt Lobo, who threw down her cane and danced on her ninetieth birthday.

DOÑA FLOR: A TALL TALE ABOUT A GIANT WOMAN WITH A GREAT BIG HEART
Doña Flor is a giant who protects her village and can communicate with animals. When the sound of a mountain lion's roar frightens the villagers, Doña Flor heads into the mountains. The other animals help her find the mountain lion; she talks to him, tames him with kindness, and becomes his friend.

HOUSE OF HOUSES
Mora's memoir of growing up in El Paso, Texas, tells the history of her family, dating back to nineteenth-century Mexico. The book contains many colorful and humorous stories about Mora's relatives and ancestors, but it also sadly recounts the death of her father.

A LIBRARY FOR JUANA: THE WORLD OF SOR JUANA INÉS
The book tells the story of young Sor Juana Inés de la Cruz, the seventeenth-century Mexican girl who studied hard to educate herself during an era when young girls were given few opportunities to go to school. Sor Juana later became a nun and author and established a library with approximately 4,000 books.

MY OWN TRUE NAME: NEW AND SELECTED POEMS FOR YOUNG ADULTS

Mora gathered and wrote the poems for this book after librarians told her that there were few poetry collections on their shelves written primarily for teenagers. The book's introduction is an essay by Mora encouraging young people to express themselves through writing.

PABLO'S TREE

Pablo's grandfather Lito planted a new tree on the day Pablo's mother adopted him. Over the years, Lito has nurtured the tree and helped it grow. Each year, Lito prepares for Pablo's visit by adding a new decoration to the tree.

THE RAINBOW TULIP

Mora wrote a children's book about her mother Stella's experience participating in the May Day parade dressed in a tulip costume of many colors; the book shows that it is hard to be different.

TOMÁS AND THE LIBRARY LADY

Tomás, the son of migrant farm workers, enjoys listening to the stories his grandfather tells him. When his grandfather runs out of stories, he urges the boy to go to the library in town to read new stories. The librarian helps Tomás discovers the world of books.

POPULAR CHARACTERS

CECILIA

Cecilia is the main character in *A Birthday Basket for Tía*. In the story, the little girl fills her aunt's birthday basket with the mixing bowl they use to make cookies, a red ball they use to play catch, a flowerpot for the flowers they grow together, the cup that holds the mint tea that Tía makes for Cecilia when she is ill, and a book that Tía reads to Cecilia.

DOÑA FLOR

Doña Flor is the giant who protects her village and tries to calm her frightened friends by digging a new riverbed with her thumb. In *Doña Flor: A Tall Tale About a Giant Woman With a Great Big Heart,* Doña Flor speaks all the languages in the world, including rattlesnake, and uses that ability to find and befriend the mountain lion who is scaring her village.

PABLO

Pablo is the little boy in *Pablo's Tree* who visits his grandfather Lito each year on his birthday. He learns that, just as his grandfather has made the tree strong by nurturing it with plenty of water, sunshine, and love, he is a lot like the tree and has also grown strong.

STELLA/ESTELITA

In *The Rainbow Tulip*, Mora based the character of the little girl Estelita on her mother, Estela Delgado, who learned how hard it is to be different when she attended the May Day parade dressed in a tulip costume of many colors.

TOMÁS

Tomás learns a lot about tigers and dinosaurs, as well as the world of books, when he visits the library in a small Iowa town. Mora based the main character in *Tomás and the Library Lady* on Tomás Rivera, the first Latino chancellor of the University of California at Riverside, who was the son of migrant farm workers.

MAJOR AWARDS

1982 Mora receives the Poetry Award, *New America: Women Artists and Writers of the Southwest.*

1983 Mora received the Creative Writing Award, National Association for Chicano Studies.

1984 *Chants* is selected for Harvey L. Johnson Book Award, Southwest Council of Latin American Studies.

1985 *Chants* is selected for Southwest Book Award, Border Regional Library Association.

1986 Mora is awarded the Kellogg National Leadership Fellowship.

1987 Mora is elected to Texas Institute of Letters; *Borders* is selected for Southwest Book Award.

1988 Mora is selected as Author of the Pass: *El Paso Herald-Post* Writers Hall of Fame.

1990 Mora receives the Poetry Award, Conference of Cincinnati Women.

1994 Mora is awarded the National Endowment for the Arts Creative Writing Fellowship in Poetry; *A Birthday Basket for Tía* selected for Southwest Book Award; *Pablo's Tree* is selected for Américas Award, Commended List, Consortium of Latin American Studies Programs (CLASP), University of Wisconsin-Milwaukee.

1995 *The Desert Is My Mother/El desierto es mi madre* is selected for the Honor Award in Nature and Ecology by *Skipping Stones* magazine.

1996 *Confetti: Poems for Children* is selected as one of the Notable Books for a Global Society by the International Reading Association; CCBC Choices by the Cooperative Children's Book Center, and Américas Award, Commended List, Consortium of Latin American Studies Programs (CLASP), University of Wisconsin-Milwaukee.

MAJOR AWARDS

1997 *House of Houses* is selected for Southwest Books Award and the Premio Aztlán Literature Award; *Tomás and the Library Lady* is selected for Américas Award, Commended List, Consortium of Latin American Studies Programs (CLASP), University of Wisconsin-Milwaukee.

1998 *This Big Sky* is named among the One Hundred Books for Reading and Sharing by the New York Public Library. *Tomás and the Library Lady* selected for the Tomás Rivera Mexican American Children's Book Award, Southwest Texas State University; Teachers' Choices by the International Reading Association; and the Honor Award in the Multicultural and International category by *Skipping Stones* magazine.

1999 Mora is awarded the Pellicer-Frost Binational Poetry Award, as well as the Carruthers Chair Distinguished Visiting Professor, University of New Mexico; *This Big Sky* is selected for Book Publishers of Texas Award, Best Book for Children or Young People, Texas Institute of Letters; Notable Children's Trade Book in the Field of Social Studies by the American Library Association; and Finalist in Children's Literature by PEN Center West.

1999–2000 *Tomás and the Library Lady* is selected for the Texas Bluebonnet Master List.

2000 Mora is selected for the Ohioana Award for Children's Literature.

2001 *My Own True Name: New and Selected Poems for Young Adults* is selected for the New York Public Library Books for the Teen Age List, and Finalist by Writers' League of Texas; *Love to Mamá: A Tribute to Mothers* is selected for the Parent's Guide Children's Media Award; Outstanding Merit, Best Children's Books of the Year by Bank Street College; and a Notable Social Studies Trade Book for Young People.

2001–2002 *My Own True Name: New and Selected Poems for Young Adults* is selected for the Tayshas Reading List, Young Adult Round Table, Texas Library Association.

2002 Mora is named a Literary Light for Children by the Associates of the Boston Public Library and selected as a member of the 100 Library Champions by the Texas Library Association's Centennial; *The Bakery Lady/ La señora de la*

MAJOR AWARDS

panadería is selected for second place by the Latino Literary Hall of Fame, Children's Picture Book Category.

2003 Mora is awarded the Civitella Ranieri Fellowship, Umbria, Italy; *A Library for Juana: The World of Sor Juana Inés* is selected for the Tomás Rivera Mexican American Children's Book Award and Américas Award, Commended List, Consortium of Latin American Studies Programs (CLASP), University of Wisconsin-Milwaukee; *Maria Paints the Hills* is selected by the Texas Institute of Letters as a finalist in the Austin Public Library Award for Best Children's Book.

2004 Mora is named a Distinguished Alumna, University of Texas at El Paso; *A Birthday Basket for Tía* is selected for Utah Governor's September Children's Book-of-the-Month; *Confetti: Poems for Children* is selected for Arizona Governor's Book Award; *A Library for Juana: The World of Sor Juana Inés* is selected for the Amelia Bloomer Project Recommended List, Feminist Task Force of the Social Responsibilities Round Table of the American Library Association.

2005 *Doña Flor: A Tall Tale About a Giant Woman With a Great Big Heart* is selected for the Golden Kite Award by the Society of Children's Book Writers and Illustrators, a Notable Book by the American Library Association, the Pura Belpré for Hispanic Literature Honor Award, and a New York Public Library Book for Reading and Sharing; *Tomás and the Library Lady* is named a selection for the Arlington Reads program.

2006 Mora is selected for the National Hispanic Cultural Center Literary Award, and received Honorary Doctorate of Letters, State University of New York (SUNY) Buffalo; *The Song of Francis and the Animals* awarded Second Place, Children's Books by The Catholic Press Association, and the Paterson Prize for Books for Young People, Special Recognition.

2007 *Adobe Odes* is awarded International Latino Book Award, Best Poetry in English; Bronze Medal in Poetry, Independent Publisher Book Awards (IPPY), and Spur Poetry Finalist, Western Writers of America.

BIBLIOGRAPHY

Books

Authors in Depth. Upper Saddle River, N.J.: Prentice Hall, 2000.

Balassi, William, John F. Crawford, and Annie O. Esturoy, eds. *This Is About Vision: Interviews With Southwestern Writers*. Albuquerque: University of New Mexico Press, 1990.

Lehr, Susan, ed. *Beauty, Brains, and Brawn: The Construction of Gender in Children's Literature*. Portsmouth, N.H.: Heinemann, 2001.

Mora, Pat. *A Birthday Basket for Tía*. New York: Macmillan, 1992.

———. *Doña Flor: A Tall Tale About a Giant Woman With a Great Big Heart*. New York: Alfred A. Knopf, 2005.

———. *House of Houses*. Boston: Beacon Press, 1997.

———. *My Own True Name: New and Selected Poems for Young Adults*. Houston, Texas: Piñata Books, 2000.

———. *Nepantla: Essays From the Land in the Middle*. Albuquerque: University of New Mexico Press, 1993.

———. *Pablo's Tree*. New York: Macmillan, 1994.

———. *The Rainbow Tulip*. New York: Viking, 1999.

———. *This Big Sky*. New York: Scholastic, 1998.

———. *Tomás and the Library Lady*. New York: Alfred A. Knopf, 1997.

Peacock, Scot, ed. *Contemporary Authors New Revision Series,* vol. 81. Farmington Hills, Mich.: Gale Group, 1999.

———. *Contemporary Authors New Revision Series,* vol. 112. Farmington Hills, Mich.: Thomson Gale, 2003.

———. *Something About the Author,* vol. 134. Farmington Hills, Mich.: Gale Group, 2003.

Rockman, Connie C., ed. *Eighth Book of Junior Authors and Illustrators*. New York: H.W. Wilson, 2000.

Periodicals

Barrera, Rosalinda B. "Profile: Pat Mora, Fiction/Nonfiction Writer and Poet." *Language Arts* 75, no. 3 (March 1998): p. 221.

BIBLIOGRAPHY

"A Birthday Basket for Tiá," *Publishers Weekly* (Aug. 31, 1992) http://reviews.publishersweekly.com/bd.aspx?isbn=0027674002&pub=pw.

Burns, Mary M. "*A Library for Juana: The World of Sor Juana Inés.*" *Horn Book Magazine* 78, no. 6 (Nov. 1, 2002): p.778.

Candelora, Versace. "Pat Mora: Bringing the Latino Experience to Children's Literature." *Santa Fe New Mexican* (Oct. 6, 1996): p. D-5.

Dearstyne, Susan. "*House of Houses.*" *Library Journal* 122, no. 7 (April 15, 1997): p. 88.

Henderson, Darwin L. "Listening to the Desert: A Conversation With Pat Mora." *Ohio Journal of the English Language Arts* 41, no. 1 (Fall 2000): p. 12.

Hopkins, Lee Bennett. "Pat Mora." *Teaching K-8* 36, no. 4 (January 2006): p. 61.

"An Interview with Pat Mora." *Journal of Adolescent and Adult Literary* 46, no. 2 (October 2002): p. 183.

Mermann-Jozwiak, Elizabeth, and Nancy Sullivan. "Interview with Pat Mora." *MELUS* 28, no. 2 (Summer 2003): p. 139.

Mora, Pat. "The Seeds of Stories." *The Dragon Lode* 18, no. 2 (Spring 2000): p. 55.

———. "A Latina in Kentucky." *Horn Book Magazine* 70, no. 3 (May 1, 1994): p. 298.

Racine, Marty. "Award-Winning Writer Glides Between Two Worlds." *Houston Chronicle* (May 30, 1999): p. 1-F.

Stuttaford, Genevieve, Maria Simson, and Jeff Zaleski. "*House of Houses.*" *Publishers Weekly* 244, no. 12 (March 24, 1997): p. 68.

Other Sources

"Creativity Survey III," Lee & Low Booktalk. Available online. URL: www.leeandlow.com/booktalk/create1b.html.

Marcovitz, Hal. Interview with Pat Mora. Oct. 25, 2006.

"Pat Mora's Interview Transcript." Scholastic. Available online. URL: http://teacher.scholastic.com/activities/hispanic/moratscript.htm.

"Pat Mora: Meet the Mentor." VHS. Scholastic, 1996.

Pereira, Aline. "Interview with Pat Mora." Paper Tigers. Available online. URL: www.papertigers.org/interviews/archived_interviews/pmora.html.

BIBLIOGRAPHY

"Sisters of Loretto Have Long Tradition in the Southwest." Borderlands, an El Paso Community College Local History Project. Available online. URL: www.epcc.edu/nwlibrary/borderlands/19_loretto.htm.

"Sor Juana Inéz de la Cruz." Available online. URL: http://oregonstate.edu/instruct/phl302/philosophers/cruz.html.

"Transcript From an Interview with Pat Mora," Reading Rockets. Available online. URL: www.readingrockets.org/books/interviews/mora/transcript.

FURTHER READING

Bayles, David, and Ted Orland. *Art & Fear.* Eugene, Ore.: Image Continuum Press, 2001.

Cameron, Julia. *Artist's Way: A Spiritual Path to Higher Creativity.* New York: Tarcher, 2002.

Gibson, Ian. *Federico García Lorca: A Life.* New York: Pantheon, 1997.

Goldberg, Natalie. *Writing Down the Bones: Freeing the Writer Within.* Boston: Shambhala Publications, 2006.

Ingalls Wilder, Laura. *Little House on the Prairie.* New York: HarperTrophy, 2007.

Lamott, Anne. *Bird by Bird: Some Instructions on Writing and Life.* New York: Anchor, 1995.

Lupton, Mary Jane. *Lucille Clifton: Her Life and Letters.* Westport, Conn.: Praeger, 2006.

Neruda, Pablo. *Memoirs.* Translated by Hardie St. Martin. New York: Farrar, Straus and Giroux, 2001.

Oliver, Mary. *A Poetry Handbook.* New York: Harvest Books, 1994.

Web Sites

"Biography of Pablo Neruda," Nobelprize.org
http://nobelprize.org/nobel_prizes/literature/laureates/1971/neruda-bio.html

City of El Paso, Texas
http://www.ci.el-paso.tx.us/

"El Día de los Niños/El Día de los Libros." ALSC: Association of Library Service to Children
www.ala.org/dia

Modern American Poetry: An Online Journal and Multimedia Companion to *Anthology of Modern American Poetry*
http://www.english.uiuc.edu/maps/

Pat Mora
http://www.patmora.com

PICTURE CREDITS

page:

- 10: © Pat Mora. Reprinted with permission.
- 15: © Pat Mora. Reprinted with permission.
- 20: © Pat Mora. Reprinted with permission.
- 23: © Pat Mora. Reprinted with permission.
- 25: © Pat Mora. Reprinted with permission.
- 28: © Pat Mora. Reprinted with permission.
- 32: © Pat Mora. Reprinted with permission.
- 38: Library of Congress, ggbain 04314
- 42: © Pat Mora. Reprinted with permission.
- 50: © Pat Mora. Reprinted with permission.
- 55: © Pat Mora. Reprinted with permission.
- 62: © Pat Mora. Reprinted with permission.
- 72: AP Images/Michel Lipchitz
- 74: © Pat Mora. Reprinted with permission.
- 79: Erich Lessing/Art Resource, NY
- 86: © Pat Mora. Reprinted with permission.
- 93: © Pat Mora. Reprinted with permission.
- 95: © Pat Mora. Reprinted with permission.
- 98: © Pat Mora. Reprinted with permission.
- 104: © Pat Mora. Reprinted with permission.

Cover: Courtesy Pat Mora/Photo by Cheron Bayna

INDEX

Abuelos (Mora), 109
activist poet, 70
Adobe Odes (Mora), 108
Agua Santa: Holy Water (Mora), 47–48, 83–84
All Soul's Day, 14, 17
American Library Association (ALA), 107
Art and Fear (Bayles and Orland), 60
artists, 82–84, 102. *See also* illustrator
Artist's Way, The (Cameron), 60
Association for Library Service to Children (ALSC), 107
Aunt Carmen's Book of Practical Saints (Mora), 33
awards, 105–106, 122–124
   Award for Creative Writing, 35
   Estela and Raúl Mora Award, 105–106
   Nobel Prize for Literature, 70, 71
   Pulitzer Prize, 69

Bakery Lady, The (Mora), 89
Basoalto, Neftalí Ricardo Reyes, 71
Bayles, David, 60
bicultural life, 40, 111
bilingualism
   advocacy of, education, 29
   character in book, 77
   in home life, 29, 109
Bird by Bird (Lamott), 60
Birthday Basket for Tía, A (Mora), 89
   aunt Lobo in, 84
   Cecilia in, 12–13, 16, 53
   childrens' version for Mora, 17–19
   dance at age 90, 12–13, 36
   publication of, 12–13
birthplace, 22
Bobbsey Twins stories, 27

Book Fiesta! El Día de los Niños/El Día de los Libros (Mora), 110–111
"bookjoy," 102–104
books
   for children, advice on, 60
   for or about Latinos, 44
   picture books, 60, 65, 77
   popular, 119–120
   scheduled releases, 118
   See also reading
border. *See* living on the border
Border Patrol, U.S., 47
Borders (Mora), 35, 44, 46
   "Secrets," 65–66
Burns, Mary M., 82
Burnside, Bill (son), 16, 33
Burnside, Cecilia (daughter), 16, 33, 105
Burnside, William H., Jr. (first husband), 33, 34

Cameron, Julia, 60
career. *See* jobs; writing
Carranza, Venustiano, 24
Chants (Mora)
   excerpt, 17, 44–45, 68
   publication of, 35
characters, popular, 121
Chavez, Cesar, 106
Chicano heritage, 43
childhood
   catching lizards in desert, 22
   favorite books in, 27
   typewriter as gift, 29–30, 73
   See also residences
"Childrens' Day/Book Day." *See* Día
Chile, 71
chronology, 112–113
Clifton, Lucille, 69
Colón, Raul, 102

INDEX

Communion (Mora), 36
"Fences," 45
communism, 71, 83–84
Confetti: Poems for Children (Mora), 65
Convent of the Order of St. Jerome, 81
culture. *See* Mexican American culture; Mexican culture

Day of the Child, The. *See* Día
Dearstyne, Susan, 94–95
Delgado, Eduardo Luis and Amelia (grandparents), 24, 92–94
Delgado, Estela (mother), 14, 21, 22, 91
   as independent woman, 84
   reading, encouragement of, 27
   as speaker, 24
   tulip costume of, 96
Delgado, Ignacia (aunt). *See* "Lobo"
Department of Homeland Security, U.S., 47
Depression, the, 23
desert
   beauty of, 78, 80
   inspiration from, 22, 54, 56, 59, 76, 111
   poems about, 35
   See also Southwest
Desert Is My Mother, The (Mora), 88
Día, 102–104, 105–108
Día de los Muertos, El, 14, 17
Día del Niño, El, 103
discrimination, 23, 48–49
Doña Flor: A Tall Tale About a Giant Woman With a Great Big Heart (Mora), 76–78
   illustrator for, 102
   wildlife in, 77–78
Doyle, Sister Mary Bernard, 30–31

education
   in Catholic schools, 30–31
   Loretto Academy, 31, 33
   medical school considered, 33
   St. Patrick's School, 26
   Texas Western College, 33
   See also bilingualism
El Día de los Niños/El Día de los Libros. *See* Día
El Paso Community College, 34
Epiphany, The, 110
Estela and Raúl Mora Award, 105

family
   children, 33
   importance of, 90, 92
   memories of, 37
   stories about, 87–89
Feast of the Three Kings, 110
feminine symbolism, 75–76
feminism, 76
Franco, Francisco, 69, 71

García Lorca, Federico, 69, 70, 71
gardener as writer, 53–57
   plant names and, 57
   tilling soil and, 54
   yard as inspiration, 54
Goldberg, Natalie, 60
Grandma Moses, 82
Grapes of Wrath, The (Steinbeck), 106
Great Depression, the, 23

haiku, 108
Hallmark, 51–52
Hepburn, Audrey, 33
Hesch, Maria, 82–83
Hispanic heritage, 43, 44
Horn Book, 13, 82
House of Houses (Mora), 89–97
   cemetery story in, 92–94
   chapter per month in, 92, 95
   family tree in, 91
   grandmother Tomasa in, 94

illustrator, 57, 59, 61, 102
immigration, 46–48
Inés de la Cruz, Sor Juana, 80–82

jobs
   college administration, 34, 35–36
   museum director, 36
   teaching, 33, 34

INDEX

See also writing
Join Hands! (Mora), 110

Kahlo, Frida, 83–84

Lamott, Anne, 60
Lamy, Bishop Jean-Baptiste, 30
landscape, 82–83. *See also* desert; Southwest
Latin America, 108, 110
Latinos
   books about, 109–110, 111
   cultural nomenclature, 43
   culture neglected, 41–44, 45–46
   demographics on, 44
   discrimination, 23, 48–49
   education and, 90–91, 101, 102
   in El Paso, Texas, 29
   Epiphany, Christmas and, 110
   experience of, 34–35
   REFORMA, 105
library
   associations, 107
   importance placed on, 27
   Latino experience, books on, 42
   in Mexico, in 1600s, 81
   See also literacy
Library for Juana: The World of Sor Juana Inés, A (Mora), 80–82
Library Journal, 94–95
Listen to the Desert: Oye al Desierto (Mora), 56
literacy, 99–111
   advocacy of, 102–103
   award for, 105–106
   "book joy," 102–104
   Día event for, 102–104, 105–108
   migrant workers and, 99–102, 106
Little House on the Prairie (Wilder), 27
living on the border
   clash of cultures, 44–46
   going back and forth, 40
   Latino culture and, 41–44
   writing about, 37, 108
"Lobo" (aunt), 11–19, 91–92
   dance at age 90, 17
   as independent woman, 84
   loving influence, 14
   storyteller influence, 13
Loretto Academy, 31, 33

Manquera, Ignacia Delgado (aunt). *See* "Lobo"
Maria Paints the Hills (Mora), 82–83
mariachi music, 29
¡Marimba Animales! (Mora), 108
Martinez, Libby (daughter), 16, 33
Maya Indians, 36
memoir. *See House of Houses*
metaphor
   desert symbolism, 78
   in memoir, 96
   in poetry, 64, 69–70
   in prose, 88
Mexican American culture, 29, 35
   clash of cultures, 44–46
   family importance in, 90
   real women in, 80
   See also Chicano heritage
Mexican culture
   Día de los Muertos, El, 14, 17
   inspiration for writing, 59
   pride in heritage, 35, 46
   in schools and libraries, 29, 41
Mexican Revolution, 14, 24, 91
Mexican War, 30
Mexico, 14, 35, 75
   Chihuahua (state), 24, 96
   Día del Niño, El, 103
   illegal immigration from, 47
   Juárez, 37
   poverty in, 45–46
Mexico-U.S. border. *See* living on the border
migrant farm workers, 99–102, 106–107
Mistral, Gabriela, 70
Mora, Cecilia (sister), 26
Mora, Chole, 25–26
Mora, Estela. *See* Delgado, Estela
Mora, Lázaro and Natividad (grandparents), 24

INDEX

Mora, Raúl Antonia (father), 21, 91
   childhood of, 92
   death of, 36–37
   education of, 24
   grandmother Tomasa of, 94
   occupations of, 22–23, 25–26
Mora, Roy Antonio (brother), 26, 105
Mora, Stella (sister), 26, 96, 105
multicultural society, 111
Museum of International Folk Art, 83
My Family/Mi Familia (Mora), 109–110
My Own True Name: New and Selected Poems for Young Adults (Mora), 58, 65, 78, 80
   "Dear Fellow Writer" essay in, 52–53, 59
   excerpt, 88
   "Family Ties," 89
   "Ode to Pizza, An," 58
   "Teenagers," 89

Nancy Drew books, 27
National Association for Chicano Studies, 35
National Association to Promote Library and Information Service to Latinos (REFORMA), 105
National Book Award, 69
nature, 76, 77–78. *See also* desert; gardener as writer
Nerinckx, Charles, 30
Neruda, Jan, 71
Neruda, Pablo, 70, 71
Night the Moon Fell, The (Mora), 75
Nobel Prize for Literature, 70, 71
nonfiction, 27, 118
nun
   consideration of life as, 30
   Convent of the Order of St. Jerome, 81
   Sisters of Loretto, 26–27, 30–31, 32–33
   See also *Library for Juana*
Nun's Story, The (film), 33

Olivares, Julián, 35
Oliver, Mary, 69
Orland, Ted, 60

Pablo's Tree (Mora), 87–88, 89
painters, 82–84
picture book, 60, 65, 77
   Desert Is My Mother, The, 88
Piñata in a Pine Tree, A (Mora), 110
poems (Mora), 117–118
   "Dear Frida," 84
   "Desert Woman," 78, 80
   "Elena," 68
   "Fences," 45
   first poem published, 35
   first three books of, 65
   "Immigrants," 46
   "Mexican Magician," 54
   "Migra, La," 47–48
   "Ode to Pizza, An," 58
   "Old Snake," 63–64, 65
   "Poet for President, A," 73–74
   "Secrets," 65–66
   "Tall Walking Woman," 66–67
   for teens, 52–53, 65
   "To My Son," 16
   "Young Sor Juana, The," 82
   See also poetry books by title
poet
   inspiration from, 69–70
   politics and, 47, 70–73
poetry
   haiku, 108
   memorization of, 30–31
   questions posed in, 66
   rhyming, unrhymed, 65
poetry, writing of
   on common subjects, 58, 108
   creating an experience, 67
   descriptive language, 66–69
   feelings and, 16
   length of poem, 67
   metaphor in, 64, 65–66
   reading aloud to self, 68
   on typewriter, 29–30
   as ultimate challenge, 67, 73
   See also writing

INDEX

Pollyanna character, 27
prose, 65, 73
publisher
   research on, 61
   working with, 57, 59
Publishers Weekly, 13, 95
Pulitzer Prize, 69

Rainbow Tulip, The (Mora), 89
   discrimination and, 48–49
   Estelita/Stella in, 40–41, 84
   origin of story, 96
reading
   to children, importance of, 101
   interest in, 26–27
   nonfiction, historical figures, 27
   picture books, 60
   summer reading clubs, 27
REFORMA, 105
residences
   El Paso, Texas, 11, 21–26, 37, 46, 73, 89, 96
   Sante Fe, New Mexico, 36, 82–83, 109
Revista Chicano-Riqueña, 35
Riggs Optical, 26
Río Grande River, 24, 37, 40, 45
Rivera, Diego, 83
Rivera, Tomás, 101–102
Robertson, Anna Mary, 82

Scarborough, Vernon (second husband), 35, 36
school. *See* education
Sisters of Loretto, 26–27, 30–31, 32–33
Sor Juana. See *Library for Juana*
Southwest, 69
   New Mexico, 82–83
   See also desert; residences
Soviet Union, 83–84
Spanish Civil War, 69, 70
Spanish language, 29, 41, 49
St. Joseph's Academy, 30–31
Stalin, Joseph, 83–84
Steinbeck, John, 106
storybooks, 117

tall tale. See *Doña Flor*
This Big Sky (Mora), 63–64, 65, 66–67
Tomás and the Library Lady (Mora), 99–102
   migrant farm workers and, 106
   real-life *Tomás* character, 101–102
Trotsky, Leon, 83

Uncle Lalo, 92–93, 94
University of California, 101, 102
University of Cincinnati, 36
University of Texas-El Paso, 33
Uno Dos Tres/One, Two, Three (Mora), 54

values, 77
Videla, González, 71
Villa, Pancho, 24

Web site, 60
Wilder, Laura Ingalls, 27
women, 75–85
   equal rights for, 81
   feminine symbolism, 78
   independent, 84–85
writing
   for children, 18–19, 73
   crediting nuns for success, 32–33
   full-time, 36
   future projects, 107–111
   groups and workshops, 60
   ideas for, 53, 59–60
   longhand draft, 54
   love of language and, 56–57
   metaphor in, 64, 69–70, 78, 88
   motivation for, 52–53
   note-taking, 56, 60
   parents' lives and, 22
   reading as preparation for, 27
   rejection letters and, 52, 61
   revisions, 56, 61, 68–69
   tips, new writers, 59–61
   See also poetry, writing of
Writing Down the Bones (Goldberg), 60

Yum! ¡Mmm! ¡Qué Rico! (Mora), 108

ABOUT THE CONTRIBUTOR

HAL MARCOVITZ is a writer based in Chalfont, Pennsylvania. His other titles in this series include biographies of Bruce Coville, R.L. Stine, Will Hobbs, Maurice Sendak, and Scott O'Dell.